REGGAE
EXPLOSION

REGGAE EXPLOSION

THE STORY OF JAMAICAN MUSIC

CHRIS SALEWICZ & ADRIAN BOOT

HARRY N. ABRAMS, INC., PUBLISHERS

Art direction and design: Dan Einzig at Mystery Design
Publishing consultant: Philip Dodd

Library of Congress Cataloging-in-Publication Data

Salewicz, Chris.
 Reggae explosion : the story of Jamaican music / by Chris Salewicz and Adrian Boot ;
 introduction by Chris Blackwell.
     p. cm.
 Includes bibliographical references and index.
 ISBN 0–8109–3789–1
 1. Reggae music Jamaica History and criticism. 2. Popular
 music Jamaica History and criticism. I. Boot, Adrian. II. Title.

ML3532 .S25 2001
781.646'097292 dc21

                                                    00–066379

Printed and bound in Italy

Harry N. Abrams, Inc.
100 Fifth Avenue
New York, N.Y. 10011
www.abramsbooks.com

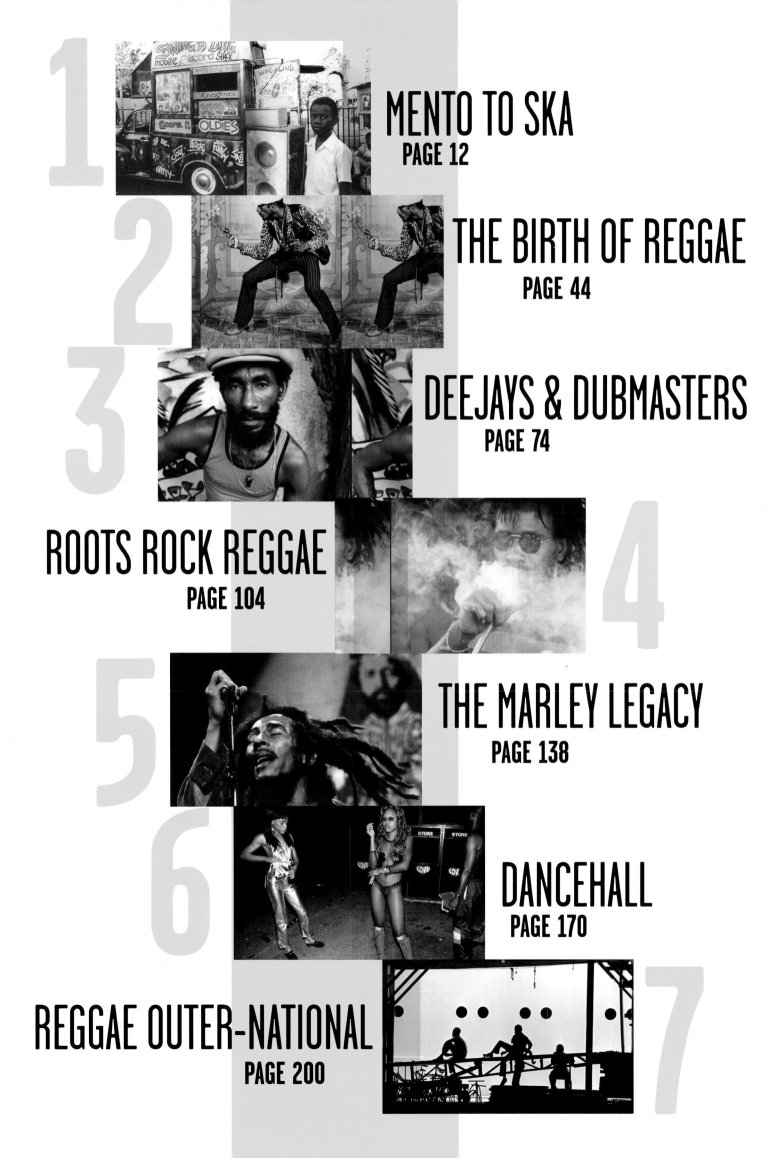

INTRODUCTION BY CHRIS BLACKWELL

For a tiny island of three million people Jamaica has had a thoroughly disproportionate effect on the course of popular music around the world: dub, re-mixes, electronic effects and - especially notable nowadays - rap music all began in Jamaica.

The sound system was another great Jamaican invention, one that now has had an effect on popular culture for over half a century. One of the ways that I financed myself when I was starting my own record label in the late 1950s was by bringing the latest, most obscure 78s down to Kingston to sell to sound systems - I would scratch off the titles on the labels so I could get a lot of money for them as no one would know who the artist was for two or three months.

What was always so important about Jamaican music was the way that it consistently honoured its African roots, much more so than American black music used to do. That really came out of the Rastafarian sensibility amongst the musicians, not only amongst people like Count Ossie's Afro-Combo - who Prince Buster had as the musicians on records like the Folkes Brothers' 'Oh Carolina' - but also in all those players who made Studio One such a definitive sound.

African rhythms have played an essential part in the life of the island; today you can hear this even in dancehall, a form of music that is totally raw and stripped down and futuristic, but whose digital rhythms at the same time are often the most ancient form of African art. The great jazz musicians of the ska era and the rude boy sounds of rocksteady made a huge contribution to Jamaican music. My favourite period, however, is the mid-1970s, the time of roots reggae. People like Burning Spear, Lee Perry, Third World, Black Uhuru, the Heptones, Peter Tosh, Bunny Wailer and Toots and the Maytals were making unbelievably great music at this time.

Of course, the standard-bearer always was Bob Marley, whose poetic words and music have gone a considerable way to making people look at their lives in a different light. Bob is seen as the archetypal Jamaican, and that's not necessarily untrue. But you mustn't forget that Jamaica is an island in which everybody is a star.

On 26th December 1950 Tom The Great Sebastian played a Christmas dance at the Forresters Hall, on the corner of North Street and Love Lane in downtown Kingston. Tom was concluding a **triumphant** first year as the **top sound system operator in Jamaica.**

MENTO

His single deck set-up, with its **enormous** selection of obscure 78 rpm records, had proved a **colossal draw for audiences all over the island.** That tropical evening saw the invention of a crowd-pleasing innovation that Tom himself, oddly enough, was not present to witness, even though he was the main draw. Launched by an inspired youngster, that innovation would eventually become central to the popular music of the late 20th century. As is the case with many crucial cultural leaps, it came about entirely by chance. For that night the

TO SKA

venue's supply of liquor ran dry, and Tom - aware that the sale of alcohol was the main source of income for a sound system operator - left the hall to fetch fresh supplies. As he did so, 'selecter' Count Machuki, still in his early teens, remained behind to continue playing the records, his customary role.

But this particular night, Machuki began 'chatting' over the shellac discs he was spinning, dropping in the kind of jive-talking phrases he had heard employed by US radio disc jockeys: "*If you dig my jive/You're cool and very much alive/Everybody all round town/Machuki's the reason why I shake it down/When it comes to jive/You can't whip him with no stick*". The crowd loved what it was hearing and Machuki earned thunderous applause.

A week later, on 2nd January 1951, Machuki repeated his feat, again on Tom The Great Sebastian's set. Tom had been preceded by Nick The Champ's 'sound'. Needing to start off hard to silence opposition chants of "The Champ, The Champ", Tom left Machuki to it, giving him the first half dozen records on which to make his vocal mark.

Again, the crowd went crazy: Nick The Champ was all but forgotten. And so Machuki began the tradition of the Jamaican deejay adding his own vocal inflections to cover any dips in a record's energy: later, customers were known to return the records they bought from Kingston stores when they discovered they had not been embellished with the kind of interjections by Machuki that they had heard at dances.

Thus began the uniquely Jamaican art of 'deejaying', a street style of music that, 30 years later, would be emulated in the United States in the form of rap music, which by the close of the 20th century was the most popular musical form in the world.

Rap is just one of the ways in which Jamaican music has culturally colonised the world. The effect it has had internationally is thoroughly disproportionate for an island with a population of only three million. Its rhythms are omnipresent, as are their cultural reverberations: reggae, rock steady, ska, and the most extreme digital forms of dancehall are part of our common musical currency. Meanwhile, around the globe, youths imitate Jamaican parlance and vocal mannerisms; and high-end couturiers purloin ragga styles for maximum catwalk impact.

The origins of most of these musical innovations can be traced to events which occurred in Jamaica in the years immediately before and after World War II, as the island began to assert its desire to gain independence following nearly two centuries as a British colony.

1938, the year before the War began, had marked twelve months of great political upheaval. A consequence of widespread workers' unrest in Jamaica was that Alexander Bustamente, a labour leader who was later to become Prime Minister, had been imprisoned for four years by the British colonial authorities. More importantly, two strong political parties had come into being - Bustamente's right-wing Jamaica Labour Party (JLP), and his lawyer cousin Norman Manley's more left-leaning People's National Party (PNP). Another side-effect of the 1938 riots, when striking sugarcane workers had been gunned down by the colonial authorities, was that ganja (the local term for marijuana), which had previously been sold on licence, was now listed as an illegal substance: clearly its users were deemed guilty of bad thinking.

This was of concern to the Rastafarians, the apocalyptic sect who believed in the divinity of Ethiopian emperor Haile Selassie I. In the immediate post-war years they had set up encampments around Kingston, especially one at Pinnacle, run by Leonard Howell, who to all intents and purposes was Jamaica's Rastafarian leader - and the new ganja laws were used with all their punitive force against the followers of Rastafari, with Howell ending up incarcerated in a mental home. The colonial authorities would also become much troubled during the 1950s when the religion's followers took to wearing their hair in long, matted dreadlocks, ostentatiously emulating a style popular with Kenya's Mau Mau freedom fighters.

The vast majority of Jamaicans, however, were not such outsiders. Most of the island's inhabitants were concerned simply with inklings of potential new prosperity. Jamaica had been ruled by the British since 1655; now, in the late 1940s, there was an undercurrent that suggested that everything was up for grabs. World War II had allowed the opportunity of significant travel for Jamaicans serving in the Allied forces, as well as bringing a large influx of foreigners, including German prisoners-of-war, into the island. People were re-defining themselves, working out who they were with a new confidence - even if the downside was the emergence of characters like Ivan Rhygin, who in 1948 went on a celebrated armed rampage, in the process becoming the outlaw hero model for the character played by the singer Jimmy Cliff in Perry Henzell's classic 1972 movie *The Harder They Come*.

FYFFES LINE

Passenger Services
to
JAMAICA

Sailings from Bristol and Southampton

ELDERS & FYFFES, LTD.
15 Stratton Street, Piccadilly, London, W.I
Jamaica Agency : 40 Harbour Street, Kingston

Jamaicas Exclusive
North Shore Resort!
Silver Seas
HOTEL

OCHO RIOS, JAMAICA
B.W.I.
276

Top centre: Marcus Garvey, in the middle, who
founded the Black Star Line to give his fellow
Jamaicans the opportunity to return to Africa.

"He layeth me down to
he leadeth me by

On the cusp between colony and independent nation, Jamaica in the 1950s was riven with deep class divisions, a heritage imported by the British colonialists.

The island was enjoying an unprecedented financial boom. Gross domestic product increased from £70 million in 1950 to £230 million in 1960, colossal growth: the bauxite companies had moved in after the discovery that the island's red soil was rich in the raw material for aluminium, and the north coast high society whirl had led to the area being developed as a luxury travel spot. But the celebrity holidaymakers hardly seemed to notice the existence of the native Jamaicans; and the more fortunate of these similarly ignored their less fortunate countrymen.

For most people life was rough. The poor grew even poorer. Unemployment was huge. Every day young men poured into West Kingston from 'country', many with no hope of earning regular money, ready material for discontent. Women came too, some trying to find work as domestic servants, others earning a living on the streets. Many found what they hoped would be salvation through immigration to the United Kingdom and Canada, while others were reduced to stowing away on boats to see where they might end up. The increasingly vocal Rastafarians would chant of what they saw as Prime Minister Norman Manley's efforts to turn them into cheap labour:

sleep on hard benches, he still factories."

Before independence was finally achieved in August 1962, Jamaica underwent a number of distinct phases: the era of the Taino Indians, the peaceful indigenous natives who were virtually extinct within 100 years of Christopher Columbus sighting the island in 1494, and invasions and rule by first the Spanish and then the British. But it was the importation of great quantities of African labour that most clearly and visibly left its mark. The music and dancing of slave celebrations, specifically that of the West African harvest ritual of Jonkanoo (alternatively known as 'John Connu', or 'John Canoe') was almost entirely African.

Jonkanoo masks (above) would bring fear to slave-owners - they were sometimes used by Maroon guerillas to infiltrate slave celebrations.

These celebrations reflected the animist origins of many of those who had been dragged in chains away from Africa. In 1725 there appeared the first published account of Christmas dancing by slaves in Sir Hans Sloane's book *A Voyage to the Islands Madera, Barbados and Jamaica*. The first mention of the word John Connu (in this case) came in 1774 in Edward Long's *History of Jamaica*: "In the towns, during Christmas holidays, they have several tall robust fellows dressed up in grotesque habits, and a pair of ox-horns on their head, sprouting from the top of a horrid sort of vizor, or mask, which about the mouth

is rendered very terrific with large boar-tusks. The masquerader, carrying a wooden sword in his hand, is followed with a numerous croud of drunken women, who refresh him frequently with a sup of aniseed-water, whilst he dances at every door, bellowing out John Connu! with great vehemence; so that, what with the liquid and the exercise, most of them are thrown into dangerous fevers; and some examples have happened of their dying." The general sense of unease for the slave-owning planters must have been increased by the fact that the paraders' disguises made them anonymous.

In Jamaica drumming was central to the slave celebrations. The drum, however, was always contentious, carrying as it did undertones of secret communication and rebellion - its sound must have been especially chilling to plantation owners dwelling in the midst of the heady atmosphere of permanent near-revolt fostered by the rebel Maroons, guerrilla fighters who, rather unsportingly, would retire to their mountainous eyries following

ambushes on British regular troops and settlers. For a time in the early 18th century, a slave owner was liable to a £10 fine if any of his slaves was found banging a drum.

Especially prominent was the celebratory sound of what became known as buru drums - or 'talking' drums, as they were known in Africa. According to *Jamaica Talk*, Frederick G. Cassidy's definitive study of the Jamaican language, the word 'buru' (or 'burru') has several related meanings: a wild dance, sometimes indecent; a low-down dancing place; and religious fanaticism - typified by 'Pocomania', the blending of West African animism with Christianity. A 'buru-man', meanwhile, is a Pocomania dancer. In the West African language of Yoruba, the word means 'wicked': appropriately, all things considered.

In addition to the buru 'talking drums', with their magical, machine-gun-like clatters and sighing spaces, there were many other forms of drumming instruments; for example, the ebo drum, which was made of a hollow tree with a piece of sheepskin stretched over it, and the bass drum (or 'kyando') which had a tonal ring around it called a 'kagga', and was made of breadfruit wood.

There were also a host of percussive instruments: such as the rattle, also known as a 'shaka', 'shakey', or 'shaker'; and the jawbone - usually that of a horse, with the teeth

loose in the sockets, across which a stick was rattled. Many other instruments were introduced into Jamaica by the island's forced immigrants. Horns were always important, especially the 'abeng', a cow horn, with which the Maroons could communicate over large distances between their hide-outs in the Blue Mountains. Also popular was conch-blowing.

Named after the dominant tribe in the part of West Africa from which it first came, the Coramantee flute - a long black reed that produces a distinctively plaintive, melancholy sound - was played with the nose. Another wind instrument was the 'benta', formed from a crooked stick. Then there was the 'balafou', a xylophone-like instrument; and the 'tambu', as the Maroons described what is known as a 'rumba box', or Cuban drum; a descendant of the African 'zanza', this uses four different-sized pieces of metal, vibrated by the thumb.

The most popular African instrument adopted in the Americas was the banjo (also known as a 'strum-strum'). According to Edward Long, it was "a rustic guitar, of four strings. It is made with a calibash; a slice of which being the largest section; and this is fastened to a handle, which they take great pains in ornamenting with a sort of rude carved work, and ribbands."

By the middle of the 18th century, the slaves had begun to adopt the genteel European dances and customs of their owners: Morris dancing, reels, the French quadrille, and even the polka became part of their repertoire. Similarly, musicians began to take up the fiddle. Frequently, there may have been an undercurrent of irony in the slaves' interpretations of such bourgeois alien forms. The extent to which the quadrille permeated Jamaican life may be gauged from the fact that the Wailers' 'Rude Boy' single, released in 1965, contained the line *"Ska quadrille, ska quadrille, ska quadrille"*.

The tourist face of Jamaica in the 1950s suggested that calypso was native to the island. But although calypso was performed in the north coast hotels, it had originated in Trinidad, in the far south of the Caribbean. Mento was Jamaica's authentic music...

Following emancipation in 1838, a substantial quantity of indentured African plantation workers entered the island. Between 1841 and 1865 some 8,000 'Free Africans' came to Jamaica, with a great many of the early arrivals settling in the eastern parish of St Thomas, particularly in the Plantain Garden River Valley. It was they who introduced the drumming rhythms with a strong emphasis on the off beat that would later become part of the rhythm of reggae.

These workers had already converted to Christianity, but it was a version of the religion that had blended interestingly with African animism, leading to the dramatic, speaking-in-tongues services of the 'religious revivalists', which comprise one of the three strands of specifically Jamaican Christianity, and that is completed by 'Kumina', a combination of Christianity and Bantu animism from southern African, and Pocomania (sects which were most prevalent in St Thomas).

Revivalism and Pocomania, says Steve Barrow, the British expert on Jamaican music, "combined African and Christian religious elements, and involved handclapping,

foot-stamping and the use of the bass drum, side drum, cymbals and rattle. The influence of both is found, alongside that of American-style Baptist church services, in the early records of the most successful Jamaican vocal group of the 1960s, the Maytals. The rhythms of Pocomania church services have also periodically been reborn in the dancehall - innovative producer Lee Perry, for example, is said to have been inspired to make his 1968 hit 'People Funny Boy' by those rhythms, heard as he was passing his church on his way to a session."

The diaspora of Jamaicans, which had begun with migration to work on the building of the Panama Canal, was well underway by the end of the 19th century. The island's migrant workers travelled throughout central America - there is a settlement of Jamaicans, still speaking their patois dialect, in Bluefields on the Atlantic coast of Nicaragua. Here, they assimilated the sounds of local musics like the tango and the samba. In Trinidad they absorbed the calypso.

The music that resulted from this amalgam was known as 'mento'. Its roots lay in the African music that was part of the Jonkanoo celebrations; to this were added Cuban rumba beats, as well as the tango and samba from Latin America, all of which were melded around European melodies. The vibrant rhythms of mento that developed were different from the more sedate style of Trinidad's calypso, although it shared that form's love of satirical and often bawdy lyrics.

The line-up of the 'mento' bands was generally banjo, hand drums, guitar, and a rumba box - often augmented by bamboo saxophone, penny whistle and sometimes a steel pan.

"Traces of mento," says Steve Barrow, "are to be found in the 'country' reggae style associated with groups like Stanley and the Turbines, the Starlights and the Maytones and, to a lesser degree, the Ethiopians, the Gladiators, and even Peter Tosh. The Meditations, one of the leading 'roots' trios of the 1970s, also nodded to the mento tradition. And at the beginning of ragga in the mid-1980s, leading producer King Jammy's two most popular deejays, Admiral Bailey and Lieutenant Stitchie, were among many who drew freely from mento imagery, for all the distance between their digital technology and the unamplified music that Stanley Motta recorded."

By the time World War II ended, however, the original popularity of mento was beginning to wane, as new sounds came into Jamaica from the United States, especially the big band music of artists like Count Basie, Duke Ellington and Glenn Miller.

Although performing mento bands had largely died out by the 50s, the music of acts like Lord Flea, Lord Fly, Lashar and Count Owen lived on, thanks to local impresario Stanley Motta, who released a stream of mento discs on his Melodisc label. Says Winston 'Merritone' Blake: "When you weren't dancing to American music, mento was the dance music. When you put on mento, the place went wild. It was our music". Latin music also made a strong contribution to the library of tunes played by sound systems, Tom The Great Sebastian being the first to play merengue.

After World War II the increasingly uncertain, guilty and repressive hold of the British colonialists was about to be shaken off. Already there were whispers of independence being granted to the island, as, in the wake of the war, was the destiny of colonies throughout the world. New times were coming. Why, weren't there calls from the mother country welcoming Jamaican workers to Britain?

This sense of optimism was reflected in the music. Jamaicans had developed a taste for American sounds when US troops had been based on the island during the War. In the late 1940s a number of local big bands were formed - for example, those of Jack Brown, Eric Dean (who employed both trombonist Don Drummond and guitarist Ernest Ranglin), and Val Bennett. Jitterbugging audiences would dance until dawn to tunes they drew on from American artists, whose bold music fitted the mood of the times.

By 1950 big bands in the USA were being superseded by newer outfits: the feisty, optimistic sounds of bop and rhythm and blues. "Since 1945," says Steve Barrow, "Jamaica has adopted and adapted American popular music forms - swing, bebop, R&B and soul - making them serve its own ends."

What was it like playing in the 1950s?

Val Bennett's band was a big enough band - I started with him when I was about 15. I began to learn the ranges of each instrument, so that was a good start for me.

I went to Eric Dean's band after that, which was really an even better band because they played a lot of music from Broadway musicals.

What were the audiences like in those days? Were they just uptown?

Music was a different thing in my young days. We had the bands that play the stock arrangements of people like Stan Kenton, Erskine Hawkins, Count Basie...

And the people used to be so conscious about this music: if they listened for those solos and a musician missed one, they knew he was not reading his music properly.

When it came to the ska days, the ability of the musicians seemed to fade because they were only concentrating on playing ska music. The Latin American music and swing music that we used to play were fading away.

ERNEST RANGLIN

The Eric Dean Orchestra plays at The Colony Club at Halfway Tree Crossroads in Kingston in 1951. The stellar line-up features many of the musicians who would have a major impact on the development of ska later in the decade, notably trombonist Don Drummond and guitarist Ernest Ranglin. Full line-up, left to right: Don Drummond, Eddie 'Tan Tan' Thornton, Lester Williams, 'Stanley', Reuben Alexander, Sam Watson, Ernest Ranglin, Eric Dean, Linton Thomas, 'Basso' and Roy Shirland.

*"Duke Reid is a type of man who really help Jamaican music to get where it is right now. He's a good man, because he used to record everybody that comes in, **never refuse a talent,** and he was the sort of man who encourage you as a youth to do good things with whatsoever you're earning now so you could be a man when you get much bigger. **And he used to pay you for your work...** He was one that paid up everything. He was a very kind and generous man, God bless his soul."*

JOHN HOLT

The means by which Jamaicans heard American R'n'B came largely through an invention unique to the island - the sound system. Sound systems were like portable discos for giants: eventually they would consist of up to thirty or forty speakers, each as large as four or six tea-chests stuck together, joined by a vast, intricate pattern of cables that seemed to be an organic growth from Jamaica's profusion of dangling liana vines. Music, which - following Machuki's night of innovation in December 1950 - would sporadically and often eccentrically be commented on by the disc jockeys spinning the records, thudded out of the speakers at a spine-shaking volume.

There had always been a large traffic of Jamaicans to the United States, a country always eager - as the United Kingdom now was - for fresh supplies of manual workers to undertake the jobs disdained by its more successful citizens. Ambitious, musically-inclined Jamaicans would return from the USA with piles of the hottest, most underground 78s. To conceal the tunes' identities, the labels would be scratched off before they were used by sound systems, the original titles sometimes completely unknown by the audiences.

The sound system dances took over Jamaica. Few people owned radios and the only way to hear the latest rhythm and blues was to go to the big outdoor dances held at what were known as 'lawns' in Kingston locations, especially in the area that came to be known as Beat Street, a downtown quarter full of venues. On North Street and Love Lane there was Forresters Hall; Chocomo Lawn was on Wellington Street; King's Lawn on North Street, and Jubilee on King Street. There was also the Bull Head Lawn on Trench Town's Central Road, and the Pioneer Lawn and the Barrel 'O' Lawn, both in Jones Town. There would be dances in indoor clubs, but also in many outdoor locations outside Kingston - Cane Hill, in a quarry by Bull Bay, and at Prison Oval in front of Spanish Town jail.

Setting up in 1950, Tom The Great Sebastian became the first significant sound system operator, especially when allied to the verbal dexterity of Count Machuki; Duke Vin, who in 1956 began the first 'sound' in the United Kingdom, would also serve as 'selecter' for him. Many, including Prince Buster, believe that Tom The Great Sebastian, who was named after a famous Barnum

"Coxsone was really the man, the man who came up with the ideas. But he couldn't play, so he would come and explain it to us. After explaining it, I always knew what the man wanted."

ERNEST RANGLIN

"Everyone started off working for Coxsone. **Studio One was like the university of reggae."**

CHRIS BLACKWELL

After the rival sound system bosses Coxsone Dodd (above and left) and Duke Reid moved into record production, Coxsone was always some lengths ahead. Yet was his willingness to turn a blind eye to their ganja-smoking part of the reason that the best musicians were drawn to him? As a former policeman, Reid would have no truck with 'herbs'.

Brothers circus performer, was the all-time giant of sound systems. "He is the man," said Prince Buster, who later ran his own system and became one of Jamaica's most innovative musicians.

The other leading sound system contenders at this time were Goodies, Count Smith The Blues Blaster, Count Joe, and Sir Nick The Champ. But they never triumphed over Tom The Great Sebastian, as would be apparent at the dances billed as sound system battles in which two or more systems would compete, each playing a record in turn: Tom would 'mash up' the opposition with the uniqueness of his tunes, straight off the plane from the USA, the sheer power of his equipment, and the originality of his deejays.

Tom The Great Sebastian reigned supreme until the rise in the second half of the 1950s of the Big Three - Sir Coxsone's Downbeat, Duke Reid's Trojan, and King

Edwards' Giant, sound systems whose supporters would follow them with football fan-like fervour. Sound clashes between the different systems started by chance when rival sounds would find themselves playing in close proximity, on neighbouring lawns: as a rival sound's tunes gusted noisily across into an adjacent dance, the only solution was to turn up the power, and hit back with an even harder record.

Soon these clashes were formalised with dances featuring two or more sound systems. All was considered fair in ensuring your set won. Sabotage was well-known, frequently involving the cutting of leads. There is one story, which is possibly apocryphal, of Duke Reid becoming enraged at the ear-splitting volume with which another sound was audaciously playing in his neighbourhood.

Going to look for this offender, Reid discovered the sounds sailing out of a state-of-the-art jukebox, gaudily replete with all manner of flashing neon lights. Drawing one of the guns he was reputedly never without, Duke Reid proceeded to fill the jukebox with a fusillade of bullet-holes, until it ceased functioning.

At the heart of Jamaican music, 'sounds' continue to the present day, as may be attested to by anyone who has attempted to get a night's sleep in Kingston on a Friday, the favourite party night. Wherever Jamaican communities have moved, sound systems have accompanied them - London's annual Notting Hill carnival features

tons of boxes, tons of house of joy,

as they are known in Jamaica.

"Sound systems came from the sounds of the earth,

from the bottom floor, and it took a long time to get respect. People didn't understand why I went to college and then went with a sound system - I was considered a worthless boy.

Without the sound system

Winston Blake started his Merritone sound system in Morant Bay, St Thomas, in the mid-1950s. Although he later moved to Kingston, Merritone was the first sound system in the eastern parish of St Thomas. Prior to that, the main social events in rural areas had been limited to events organised by churches or political parties, although 'nine nights' - the local term for funeral wakes - were always "great events", declares Blake.

Blake's first experience of a 'sound' was the one he would hear from the bus that took him back from school in Kingston to St Thomas: the Challoners sound system, run by a Mr Chin at his record shop in midtown Halfway Tree. Later Winston acquainted himself with as many of the reigning 'sounds' as he could, including Duke Reid, Sky Rocket, Blue Mirror - and King Edwards, who arrived in 1956 "with a boom... One of the heaviest sound systems I've ever heard. You could be ten miles away and get the beat in your head when Edwards was playing".

Local clubs still catered to live music. Some of the most popular were Sugar Hill, Glass Bucket and Bournemouth, one of the great nightspots of Jamaica, where the Skatalites had a residency. For a long time, dancing at a 'sound', rather than in a nightclub, was considered extremely downmarket.

When Blake set up Merritone, he began with a Philips 20-watt amplifier, having first made sure it ran on batteries, because in the country areas where he first played there was frequently no electricity. He used a Garrard turntable, with brass needles screwed into the arm to play 78 rpm discs, American records acquired from Duke Reid, Coxsone Dodd, stores like Chin's or One Eye, or bought from Jamaican farmworkers who travelled to the United States on short-term contracts; plenty of records would also change hands in brothels, brought in by sailors. Alternatively they could be bought by mail-order, specifically from two stations broadcasting out of Tennessee - Randy's and Ernie's, though the records were often smashed by the time they arrived.

Sound system clashes began when two or more 'sounds' were playing in the same area. "Up to half a dozen steel speaker-horns would be set up pointing into the other dance. People would wait and see what each sound was playing - one record could determine where an audience went on a Saturday night." In most cases, it was the deejay and the originality of his 'toasting' that made the difference. Machuki and King Stitt were the main deejays for Coxsone; for Duke Reid, it was Cuttins and Cliffie, while Lord Koos had Hickey Man.

Each area had its own special sounds. "Montego Bay had Quaker City, which was like a thundering sound. In Spanish Town you had two big sounds: Moody's and Lord Ruddy's. They dominated St Catherine - you were in Ruddy's or Moody's territory. Everyone had a territory."

One name, however, came along to challenge everyone, remembers Blake. "When Prince Buster came on the scene I don't think any words can describe his entry. Buster really ran the top sounds into the ground. He came, he saw, he conquered. When he played, anything in his path he'd throw it down. A glorious era."

here would be no Jamaican music."

Winston Blake

"Before Bob Marley there was only Prince Buster - no one else on that scale."

DAVID RODIGAN

Did you actually work for Coxsone?

I didn't work for Coxsone. Coxsone was under pressure from Duke Reid bad men and they came to my corner and asked me and my friends to help them against Duke Reid men.

Were you already a deejay at this point?

No, I was a singer. I was singing in clubs and things. Duke Reid was on George Street. But we had this gang of boys on my corner that was all followers of Tom The Great Sebastian. Tom The Great Sebastian was the greatest sound man of all time. He was never defeated. He left Beat Street because of the violence and moved to another part of town and made much more money there. For some reason this man has not been given any credit. It hurts me: that's why I always speak of him. Tom The Great Sebastian is the man.

In 1938 the first serious social unrest of the century broke out in the British colony of Jamaica. As the country staggered from the effects of the worldwide depression, rioting broke out across the Caribbean island, and on 24th May, Kingston was almost rent asunder. Then, at the heart of this hell, an incident of great courage took place. Sir William Alexander Bustamente, the leader of the Jamaica Labour Party, stepped in front of police pointing firearms at demonstrators. "Shoot me," he offered himself, "and save the innocent people of Jamaica." Bustamente subsequently became the island's first Prime Minister.

It was on this auspicious day that one Cecil Campbell was born, and it was hardly surprising that as a consequence he should have been given the nickname of 'Buster'.

Was he before the other sound system operators?

Tom was like 1949-50 - in them times Coxsone and Duke Reid weren't even on the scene. Coxsone came from country. Tom did deejay himself, and one of Tom's deejays was Count Machuki. Another one was Duke Vin who became a very popular man in London. [Duke Vin, who ran a celebrated shebeen in West London, is widely cited as having been the first sound system operator in Britain.] But Tom The Great Sebastian was the start in Jamaican music and nobody wants to give him credit. Ask the people: they will tell you that Tom The Great Sebastian wasn't rowdy dance. When he playing against Count Nick or Count Buckrum, they would match music to music - not like Duke Reid who would come with a bunch of bad man, chuck out people, stab up people and mash up sound system.

So Duke Reid was like a gangster?

Being an ex-policeman, Duke Reid
knew a lot of criminals who he had sent to prison
himself. He was located on a corner called Pink
Lane, in West Kingston near Charles Street - it was
one of the baddest corners in Jamaica at the time.
All these old prisoners flocked around him. He
challenged Tom a couple of times and then found
out that he was no match. So he decided now to use
the bad men to mash up Tom. They started fights
and everything and Tom wasn't a man of fight.
So Tom just pack up his sound and say he's gonna
leave Beat Street, and went to a place called Silver
Slipper in Crossroads - a nicer place, all the matinee
crowd running behind him. Duke Reid moved into
Forresters [Forresters Hall, on the corner of North
Street and Love Lane] as the main thing after Tom
left. But he wasn't another Tom.

What happened to Duke Reid
now, he was ruling through violence and he had
a lot of followers in the criminal world. And he
had a lot of girls working for him: he'd buy special
clothes for them to wear at the dance - there was
one named Duddah: she controlled all the rest of
the girls for him.

*As well as using guns and violence, Duke Reid was
said to use obeah [Jamaican voodoo]: did he let people
know this?*

No, he tried to hide it. But once he
went all the way to Chicago [many of the principal
obeah textbooks are published out of Chicago] to
see a man called Lawrence to build with him to try
and put me out, you know. My grandmother at an
early age had taught me about those things and so
they don't affect me - that's for illiterate people.
Duke Reid failed: him can't make ya house just
catch a fire.

In Jamaica a lot of people
believe in obeah business. I worship
one God, not two or three. There can only be one
master. I don't think I can speak for all people in
Jamaica but I just speak for myself. I paid the dues,
I came to defend the people's rights. I didn't just
sing about it: I went out to fight it against the
power and the government.

Reared amidst the grinding poverty of West Kingston, Buster
showed himself to be a blend of intelligence, talent and
toughness. A keen sportsman, he took to boxing from the age of
seven, often at a street corner location outside a restaurant owned
by a Mr Jenkins. It was this Mr Jenkins, keen to boost the self-
esteem of this wiry, fearless little fighter, who added the title of
Prince to his name. Prince Buster was therefore in line with so
many Jamaican performers of the 1940s and 50s who assumed
mock aristocratic sobriquets.

When he was twelve, Buster became a regular at the sound
system of Tom The Great Sebastian, one of the earliest 'sounds'
in Jamaica. Later Coxsone, as Clement Dodd became known,
sought assistance from Prince Buster and his gang of youths
against Duke Reid's attempts at disruption. Buster, who had
begun singing, would occasionally act as deejay. In 1956 he
opened Buster's Shack, his first record store, just off Parade, the
heart of downtown Kingston.

After falling out with Coxsone over money, Prince Buster
decided to set up his own sound system, The Voice Of The People,
in 1958, calling in financial favours from all over Kingston. To
compete with the established 'sounds', with their discs straight off
the plane from the USA, Buster decided to record local musicians,
renting the studio at JBC, the Jamaican Broadcasting Corporation.
To this end, he created a group comprised of some of the island's
most formidable talents: 'Drumbago' on drums, Jah Jerry on
guitar, Lester Sterling on alto sax, Rico Rodriguez on trombone,
Eric 'Monty' Morris on vocals.

A mixture of American and Caribbean music, the resulting
music provided some of the first rumblings of what came to be
known as ska: at the first session he also recorded a tune called
'Oh Carolina' by The Folkes Brothers, which was a huge
worldwide hit in 1993 when it was covered and substantially
sampled by Shaggy. (Later the track became the subject of court
litigation, with Buster eventually losing a battle for the copyright
of the song).

The acetates or dubplates that emerged from the first sessions
rocketed Buster's 'sound' to the premier position in Jamaica. As a
consequence, he came under frequent attack from Duke Reid's
badman gang, once being stabbed in the back with an ice-pick,
and on another occasion having his skull cracked open.

Released as singles, these songs invariably sold well. In
England, moreover, where songs with his own vocals were
released on the Melodisc label, Buster's ska tunes -'30 Pieces
Of Silver', 'Judge Dread', 'The Ten Commandments Of Love', and
'Al Capone', for example - were championed by the emergent
Mod movement.

Today, the very likeable Prince Buster lives in north Miami, in a
middle-class black suburb. His home has a swimming-pool and a
recording studio: he seems to have miles of tape of unreleased
recorded music, and he tours Japan frequently.

You seemed to become a musical force in Jamaica very quickly at the end of the 1950s. Is that how it happened?

Those people who come to dance at Coxsone dance, they didn't see it as
Coxsone, they see it as my sound. I had this large following of people following me all the time. So when I decided to leave Coxsone and make a sound, all these people just move with me, y'unnerstan'?

What date is this?

Some time in 1958. The thing that mess
them up was that I built up bigger sound than Duke Reid ever have, and everybody wonder where I get the money from because them couldn't believe this when they come and see the sound. I always tell them is because somebody up there love me. There was this place called One Heart along Church Street that we used to sell records to and those people used to sell speakers. I went to the lady and she call her husband and t'ing and tell him we were going to make a sound system and t'ing. And him tell her 'Give Prince anything he needs, man, everything him need'. I did have some money and I put that in. But he gave me more speakers than anybody had now and as I work the dance me pay back my promise and I do it. If I had come with a smaller sound, it wouldn't make sense. I came bigger than them as the first attraction, and the people was there with me - Prince Buster, The Voice of The People. But you must understand that I'm just taking over Duke Reid, not even Coxsone. Taking over from Duke Reid wasn't a simple thing 'cos this man had his men spot to kill me night and day.

He was like a wild man. You must
unnerstan', before Duke Reid died [of cancer, in 1975], he and I became good friends. Man wouldn't believe that because funny to know that I and Duke look in the past and he realise I beat him and he was manly enough after all the war to accept.

So in the end Duke Reid proved himself an honourable man?

I'm saying this to you. I learn a lot from
Duke Reid, even the violence - and he played a lot of dirty games, a lot of nasty dances. But I was young, and I learned by those things and now when I grow older, I say, yeah, Duke Reid was a good school for me. After he came out of the violence he was just a nice man. In the sound system times he was just possessed by what was going on. He didn't wear the gun on his hip much neither. You see, the man died, so you get to weigh up his good and his bad and I see the bad was bad, but the good was good.

"When Buster came on the scene, he took care of everybody's business."

WINSTON BLAKE

Although there was clearly an ironical purpose in the aristocratic titles adopted by so many sound system bosses, it was also the only way non-white Jamaicans could possibly hope to aspire to such dizzy heights. Arthur 'Duke' Reid The Trojan took his name from the Bedford Trojan truck in which he transported his equipment - the money for his battery of equipment came from the Treasure Isle liquor store owned by his family, which had been set up when his wife won the national lottery in 1953. His sound system had first been developed to play at the liquor store, a means employed by several alcohol-vending competitors - including his rival Clement 'Coxsone' Dodd - to draw in customers.

Reid in particular was a legendary figure. Sporting a pair of revolvers in his belt, from which he would indiscriminately loose off shots, he was more inclined to destroy the opposition through violence than talent - although his onstage performances were indubitably creative: clad in an ermine robe, a gold crown atop his head, he would be carried onto the stage by the crowd.

To Duke Reid, who began operating about four years after Tom The Great Sebastian, may be attributed the genesis of much of the gangland-like behaviour that became a later feature of the Jamaican music business. Instead of mashing up the sound system opposition by playing the heaviest, loudest tunes, he would simply charge in to opposition dances with his gang, beating up people or stabbing them and destroying their equipment. A former policeman, Duke Reid would employ some of the criminals he had personally sent to prison; and at dances he would even have gangs of tough, sexy women, all dressed in the same uniforms, controlled by a female lieutenant called Duddah. In truth, this violence was thoroughly unnecessary: for Duke Reid's real power lay in his 'tons of house of joy', as sound system speakers were referred to. And if sheer volume of sound didn't work, Reid was always partial to resorting to a spot of 'obeah', as Jamaican voodoo was known.

Tom The Great Sebastian desired to have no part in this newly violent musical world. Tom had had his headquarters on the corner of Pink Lane, one of the toughest corners in Jamaica: near Charles Street in West Kingston, it was part of the area known generically as Beat Street. Needing to move away from this newly dangerous part of downtown Kingston, Tom The Great Sebastian packed up his sound and set up permanent residence in a venue called The Silver Slipper in Crossroads. With music fans no longer intimidated by the atmosphere around the venue, he found he made far more money than down in Beat Street.

Soon, however, there came a contender for Duke Reid's crown: the Sir Coxsone Downbeat sound system, which took its name from the Yorkshire cricketer Coxsone and was run by one Clement Seymour Dodd, whose family was also in the liquor store business. Coxsone employed Prince Buster as one of his main disc jockeys - Buster's former occupation of boxer also ensured that he was a considerable deterrent to the thugs run by Reid. Dodd, who was born in 1932, first played music outside his parents' liquor store on a 30-watt Morphy Richards record-player: his father was a dock foreman who would help him get records from visiting sailors.

After building speaker boxes for early sound systems, Coxsone started up his own 'set'. When he began going to New York to purchase records, he would bring back jazz but also the R'n'B of B.B. King and T-Bone Walker. By 1957 Coxsone had three 'sets' touring Jamaica. That year both he and Duke Reid started to record acetates for use solely at their sound system dances, and soon both Coxsone and Duke Reid began recording songs by local artists specifically for use on their respective systems. The law of supply and demand showed itself to be inescapable, and out of this - as well as Coxsone's realisation that American record companies like Imperial and Modern didn't seem to notice when he blatantly pirated their material - was born a unique cornerstone of the Jamaican recording industry.

Many of the foundations for this already had been laid. In 1958 a young white Jamaican called Chris Blackwell had begun to put out records, mainly pressed up in the form of 78 rpm releases, of local artists on a label that he called Island Records: his first hit was Laurel Aitken's 'Boogie In My Bones', a classic example of Jamaican 'blues', with Aitken aping the vocal style of the Memphis artist Roscoe Gordon. Another young man was a rival - Edward Seaga, a Harvard-educated anthropologist, who was releasing Jamaican tunes on his West Indies Records Ltd (WIRL) label.

Coxsone's earliest recordings were issued only as sound system acetates, but in 1959 he decided to release his productions on seven-inch 45 rpm records to the retail market. Coxsone Dodd's first commercial session was held at Federal studio, with Alton Ellis recording 'Muriel', a prison ballad, accompanied by Clue-J's Blues Blasters as backing group. Coxsone then began recording at the Jamaica Broadcasting Corporation's studio with several vocalists, again backed by Clue-J and the Blues Blasters, a group made up of Cluett Johnson (bass), Roland Alphonso (sax), Ernest Ranglin (guitar), Rico Rodriguez (trombone) and Theophilus Beckford (piano).

The heroes of Jamaican sound systems lived on in the UK: Lloyd Coxsone, the don of British sound systems, named himself and his sound in tribute to Clement 'Coxsone' Dodd.

Gay

JAMAICA

INDEPENDENCE

TIME

ST JAMAICAN SKA GROUPS

SKA

Treasure Isle L/P

The joyous sound of ska provided the soundtrack to independence for Jamaica. The island finally shook off colonial rule on 6th August 1962, when constitutional documents were handed over to Prime Minister Alexander Bustamente by Princess Margaret on behalf of Queen Elizabeth II. A new journey had begun.

Ranglin was performing with Cluett Johnson, who played double bass, and with whom the guitarist enjoyed a creative partnership.

Dodd had quite specifically created a houseband to achieve a consistency of sound. Other backing groups he used included Hersan and the City Slickers, Aubrey Adams and the Dew Droppers, Count Ossie and the Warrickas, Ken Richards and the Comets, and the Coxsonairs. At various times Coxsone also used the Soul Defenders (whose vocalists were Freddy McKay and Joseph Hill), the Soul Vendors, and the Studio One Band, with the rhythm section of Bagga Walker on bass, Leroy 'Horsemouth' Wallace on drums and Asher on keyboards. Prominent in both of these latter groups were Rick 'Rickenbacka' Frater and Jah Privy on guitars - the records on which they initially played were what became known as 'Jamaican Blues' records, New Orleans-style rhythm and blues.

Clement Dodd had similar attitudes to those of Berry Gordy at Motown. As his recording operations developed, he modelled his early business style on American labels; he asked for exclusive contracts and wanted to push artists as being on his label: he made sure, for example, that the Wailers had their gold lamé Beatle jacket suits. His rhythms always had a rough edge; from his days pushing his Downbeat set, he had learned what moved a crowd at a dance. Whereas the sound of labels like Beverley's, Federal, and even Duke Reid suggested aspirants to a more exclusive lifestyle, Clement Coxsone Dodd's Studio One, based in Trench Town, was the sound of the man in the street. On first hearing, early Studio One records have an apparently strange mix: but it is one that sounds very

Although the group backing Alton Ellis on 'Muriel' was known as Clue-J's Blues Blasters, Ernest Ranglin was to all intents and purposes its leader. A professional jazz guitarist influenced by musicians such as Charlie Christian and Django Reinhardt, Ranglin had played in the big bands of Eric Dean and Val Bennett before being hired by JBC Radio in 1958 as their staff guitar-player. At the same time

different when an open-air surrounding is absorbing the deep bass frequencies - the Downbeat sound system almost always played out of doors.

Duke Reid's first release was the mento 'Penny Reel' by Lord Power. "He would have a 'box', a speaker, downstairs in the store so he could hear exactly what's going on upstairs in the studio," John Holt remembered of working with Reid when he had set up his Treasure Isle studio. "So if anything is goin' that he doesn't really appreciate then he would come upstairs and fire a lot of blank shots. He used to wear two guns, and a Winchester 73 across his shoulder and a big hat, cowboy-lookin' hat. He was really a different person but I like him very much."

Both Dodd and Coxsone were assisted in their search for new artists by the regular talent shows that would take place on the island, especially *Opportunity Hour* with Joseph 'Vere Johns' Veerjohns.

"He's got sort of forgotten," said Holt, "but we don't forget him 'cause he was the one who took the shakes, like the nervousness, out of our knees, like Alton Ellis, Bob Marley and the Wailers on a whole, Dennis Brown, Ken Boothe, Marcia Griffiths and many other artists. He's the man who really groomed Jamaican talent during that time, about 1958.

"These were live theatre shows, at the Majestic Theatre, Ambassador Theatre, Palace Theatre and so forth. They also had *Opportunity Knocks* on RJR radio Saturday, one o'clock, different acts, but sometimes some of us get involved in that because we need the prize - and the prize was money and trips. And if you win the finals the guys will say, 'Well, John Holt, from tonight you are now a professional singer'. 'Just out of Reach' was the song I sang that night, it was done up originally by Solomon Burke and it do me some good. Then I made a song for Leslie Kong's Beverley's Records, which was titled 'Forever I Will Stay'."

One Sunday morning in 1959 bass-player Cluett 'Clue-J' Johnson and Ranglin were requested by Coxsone Dodd - in a surprisingly formal manner - to meet him at the liquor store he ran in Love Lane. "I need something to get away from this blues," he told the two master musicians, bemoaning the manner in which Jamaican music was imitating contemporary American black music.

In the store's backyard they sat down and worked out the recipe for a new sound; they sought a formula for a music that was distinctly Jamaican whilst retaining its roots in the R'n'B and popular jazz that beamed down into Jamaica from radio stations in the southern American states. Ska, the music that resulted from that Sunday morning session, was a shuffle boogie rhythm of the type popularised by artists like Louis Jordan and Erskine Hawkins; the unexpected emphasis on the off-beat only emphasised its addictive flavour. An apocryphal explanation of the galloping sound of ska was that this was a replication of the way music on those southern radio stations would fade in and out. Ernest Ranglin, however, has a simpler explanation. "We just wanted it to sound like the theme music from one of those westerns that were on TV all the time in the late 1950s." The term 'ska' was an abbreviation of 'skavoovee', a popular catchphrase of the time, a term of approval, for the use of which Clue-J was famous. (Coxsone for his part addressed almost every man he encountered as 'Jackson', for which verbal eccentricity he was at least equally renowned.)

The next day Coxsone went to the JBC radio studios, and started trying out examples of this new music to be tested out on his sound system. The first ska record to be released, after it had received tumultuous acclaim at dances, was 'Easy Snappin'' by Theophilus Beckford. It featured pianist Beckford on vocals, Clue-J on bass, Ian Pearson on drums, Ken Richards on guitar, Roland Alphonso on tenor sax and trombonist Rico Rodriguez.

From the country parish of Manchester, Ernest Ranglin was taught guitar at a young age, especially influenced by the jazz playing of Charlie Christian. A superlative musician of great and beautiful natural talent, he played with the notable Jamaican big bands of the late 1940s, first with Val Bennett and then with Eric Dean and Count Boysie, all the while developing into the jazz musician he would become. Acquainted with Coxsone Dodd and Cluett 'Clue-J' Johnson, he played with the bassist in 1959 on several of the shuffle-boogie records that Johnson's Blues Blasters put out on Coxsone's new Studio One label. Throughout the ska era he was greatly in demand, arranging many of Coxsone's tunes, including those of the young Bob Marley. Moving to London, where - following a long residency at Ronnie Scott's - he was voted jazz guitarist of the year in 1964 in Melody Maker, Ranglin arranged 'My Boy Lollipop' by Millie, a tune that was to sell over seven million copies worldwide. Returning to Jamaica, he became musical director of Duke Reid's Treasure Isle studio. Living for a long time in Miami, from where he pursued his career as a jazz guitarist, Ernest Ranglin has more recently returned to live in Jamaica, continuing to release such superb records as 1996's *Below the Bassline*.

Everyone you speak to from the early 1960s in Jamaica seems to claim to have invented ska. But Ernest Ranglin has a more reasonable case than most.

"I'm the real foundation member of ska music.

Clue-J was my bass-player. Anywhere you see Clue-J and the Blues Blasters it is my music. How the Skatalites formed was that Jackie Opel, the singer, came from Trinidad, and Coxsone wanted me to play with him - he was a fine singer. And after we finished the LP the guys said, **'Since we are all together, we are a fine aggregation'.** And that's how they formed the band, the Skatalites. I was still at the studio because I was one of Coxsone's musical arrangers. If I am not there when they are recording, I am there at the master 90 per cent of the time to see that maybe the bass is not good, or the piano - take it out, clean it up.

With Coxsone, we came to a meeting one Sunday, because listening to all these Louis Jordan and Bill Doggett people, it's the same shuffle rhythm. So we just wanted to put more **emphasis on the 2nd and 4th beat**, which makes it a little more personal to us, our trademark. So that's where the whole thing came from."

The record was a big hit, the first ska hit, on Coxsone Dodd's Worlddisc label; its B-side was 'Silky', featuring Ernest Ranglin on his own composition.

The sound of ska was to provide the soundtrack of the independence finally granted to Jamaica on 6th August 1962. Beneath its innocent optimism, the music was frequently wistful and elegiac; horn-led, its minor chord-loaded instrumental tunes came replete with the Rastafarian thinking of many of the musicians who played it.

Many of these were employed by Coxsone Dodd. When Federal bought a two-track studio, Coxsone purchased their original one-track from them and installed it in the new premises that he took over in 1963 at 13 Brentford Road, in a former nightclub known as The End. This became the home of the Studio One label. After a while, Federal graduated to an eight-track machine, and in turn Coxsone purchased their two-track.

With Ernest Ranglin as arranger, and a teenage boy called Bob Marley as talent scout, the sound system operator was soon recording ceaselessly; it would be two years before Duke Reid opened his own studio. Several of the musicians who recorded for Coxsone - including keyboards man Jackie Mittoo, tenor saxophonist Tommy McCook, bassist Lloyd Brevette and drummer Lloyd Knibbs - became the backbone of a group who largely worked out of Studio One. Soon they included the master 'bone-player Don Drummond, the tenor sax-player Roland Alphonso, and trumpet-player Johnny 'Dizzy' Moore. Several of these artists had been pupils at Kingston's Alpha

Boys' School, Jamaica's goldmine of musicians.

In 1964 they officially formed into the Skatalites, a Tommy McCook play on words inspired by Soviet space satellites, and backed almost every important artist of the time; their tune 'The Guns of Navarone' was a huge club hit in the UK. Although together for only just over a year - they disbanded in August 1965, following a show at a police dance in Runaway Bay - the group's name remains synonymous with the ska genre.

Ska, too, has proved seemingly immortal. In the late 1970s it was revived by Jerry Dammers' 2-Tone movement, and - courtesy of such acts as the Specials, Madness, the Beat, and Selecter - dominated the UK charts for much of 1979 and 1980.

In April 1979, The Specials, under the supervision of its inspired leader Jerry Dammers, released their first single on their own label, 2-Tone, distributed through Rough Trade. The A-side was a song called 'Gangsters', a re-working of the Prince Buster classic 'Al Capone'. On the flip was a tune by another act altogether, the Selecter, with a number called precisely that: 'The Selecter', the Jamaican term for sound system record spinners. 'Gangsters' was an immediate success. The cartoon rude boy - Walt Jabsco, as he was known - drawn for the label helped establish the look of the movement: tight-fitting mohair suits and porkpie hats, as worn some fifteen years previously by both Jamaican immigrant rude boys and British Mods. The image of Walt Jabsco was based on the picture of Peter Tosh on *The Wailin' Wailers*, the classic Studio One LP on which the Wailers were backed by the Skatalites. "It isn't necessarily just a ska thing," Jerry Dammers explained. "What we want to do is develop ska into something almost unrecognisable in much the same way as the Stones did with R'n'B in the '60s: we're trying to maintain the identity of the label in the way that Stax or Tamla had an identity. The basic thing is Anglo-Jamaican music. It's trying to integrate those two."

From north London came another group whose sound was based on ska - the perky and very funny Madness, who would go on to become one of the UK's most successful singles groups. But most of these new groups came from Britain's equivalent of Detroit - Birmingham and Coventry, the two cities that made up the heart of the UK Midlands' Motown. Whilst Coventry had supplied the Specials and Selecter, Birmingham provided the Beat and Dexys Midnight Runners.

In the 1990s, ska became exceptionally popular again in the United States, its provenance often being traced back no further than the 2-Tone label. In Japan, meanwhile, the Ska Flames carried the galloping beat.

Opposite: The multi-racial 2-Tone movement founded by Jerry Dammers (on far left, with fellow Specials Lynval Golding and Sir Horace Gentleman) was an off-shoot of the punk-reggae fusion which had important cultural repercussions. This page: The rum bars of Jamaica's Port Antonio were rather more basic than anything you might find in the Specials' home base of Coventry.

'Do The Reggay' by the Maytals was released in August 1968, on Leslie Kong's Beverley's label. The single's title was the first published use of the word, which naturally has led to it being **celebrated as the first reggae record**. In the anarchic world of Jamaican academia, this spelling at first was

THE BIRTH

relatively commonplace: there was a group called the **Reggay Boys,** and Byron Lee and the Dragonaires had LPs entitled **Reggay Eyes** and **Reggay Blast Off**. The actual origins of the word remain obscure: producer Clancy Eccles, for example, claims to have invented the term - 'streggae' is said to have been a slang expression for a prostitute, and it has also been suggested that 'reggae' is a corruption of the word 'ragged', which would provide the word with appropriate 'street' connotations. Earlier in 1958 the Maytals had released another record, '54-46 (That's My Number)', the group's first single after an enforced absence of two years.

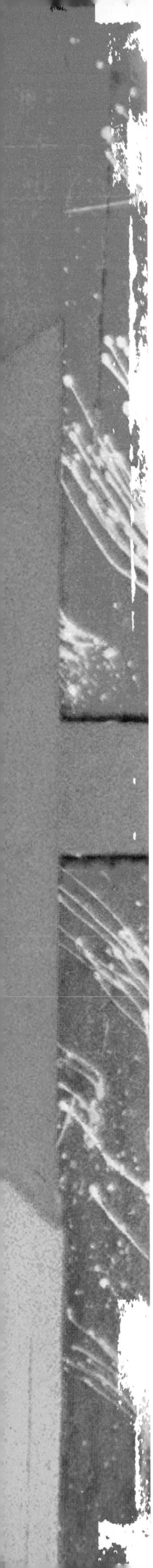

OF REGGAE

It told, with a powerful downbeat, the prison experiences of lead singer Toots Hibbert, a 24-month term he had served for possession of marijuana. This heartfelt tale, which helped to create one of the greatest Jamaican singles ever, was enhanced by a rhythm that fused the old and the new, rocksteady and reggae.

At the time 'Do The Reggay' was released, it was the lilting, sensuous sound of rocksteady that had been the leading form of Jamaican music for the previous two years or so, since the middle of 1966. Following seven or eight years when the boogie beat of ska had dominated the music of Jamaica, its rhythm had begun to change: the bassline started to break up, coming in shorter, more pronounced patterns of notes than it had for ska.

Rocksteady was literally a steadier arrangement of the beat. Its origins have been given a probably apocryphal explanation: that an unusually hot summer in 1966 rendered impossible the faster dance movements of ska. Whatever the reason, by that autumn, rocksteady was the pre-eminent sound emerging from Kingston's recording studios.

With its swing and bop influences, ska had always had a feel that was essentially 'grown-up'. Rocksteady, however, was languid and sensuous - and sounded like trouble. It was little surprise that it was taken up by the cooler-than-cool, hotter-than-hot, uniquely Jamaican youth tribe known as the 'rude boys'. From rock'n'roll's quasi-juvenile delinquents through to rap music's urban chic gangstas, an important element in the selling of any new musical form has been that it should create its very own youth cult - and the rude boys were the most extreme version yet to emerge, a product of the already somewhat exaggerated nature of Jamaica itself.

Their origins were clear. Jamaica had become an independent nation in 1962, but this independence was largely nominal. Reliance on the United Kingdom had been replaced by a need to lean on the whims of multi-national corporations in the United States and Canada, specifically those that ran the bauxite industry, which - in exchange for tearing apart and turning large chunks of the gorgeous Jamaican landscape into ugly strip mines - provided the raw ingredients for the manufacture of aluminium. Huge numbers of young people had migrated to Kingston from the countryside. Unemployment or under-employment was the norm, and many of them eked out an approximate living in the shanty-towns and slums of west Kingston.

The notion of the Rude Boy may be seen as a metaphor for Jamaica itself. But it also suggests the arrogance required to stand tall in a social situation where the insurance policy of a welfare state is utterly non-existent. The rude boys personified the blurred dividing line between reality and life on the silver screen that is so quintessentially Jamaican, by modelling themselves on the heroes or villains of cowboy films (especially the ultra-violent spaghetti westerns that first appeared in the mid-1960s) and Hollywood's juvenile delinquents. Armed with their favourite weapon, the ratchet-knife - which could be swung open at lightning speed - the anarchic rude boys were like a vision of a dystopian future.

Their influence also extended overseas, transported to wherever there were Jamaican communities; with their porkpie hats and mohair suits, they were one element of influence for the English mods, whose seaside riots in the mid-1960s shook the UK establishment.

For his film *The Harder They Come* director Perry Henzell modelled his rude boy hero, played by Jimmy Cliff, on Ivanhoe 'Rhygin' Martin, one of Jamaica's earliest and most celebrated badmen, who had gone on an armed rampage in 1948. 'Rhygin' has two meanings, either of which could apply to the rude boys: vigorous, spirited, and wholehearted; and cross, wild and raging.

The rude boys were an outgrowth of the 'dance crashers' who had been employed by sound system bosses from the 1950s onwards to mash up the equipment and enjoyment of their rivals. Such a readily mobilised mob also offered opportunities for politically ambitious individuals, such as Edward Seaga, who had founded WIRL Records in 1958 and was now a minister for the Jamaica Labour Party (JLP). Politics in Jamaica operate at the most basic of levels: if your Member of Parliament is voted out of office, you are likely to lose the job and home that he has provided for you, his supporter - hence the desperate, occasionally murderous levels to which elections can descend.

Rude boys outa jail? The cinema sources of rude boy style - part western hero, part Hollywood gangster - were immediately apparent.

The social origins of the rude boys were distinctly downtown; the cauldron of Trench Town, for example, threw up more than its fair share. Largely because of its location close to downtown Kingston, the area became a power-point to which displaced souls were drawn. "When I left May Pen," remembered Toots Hibbert, "I went to Trench Town - automatically, Trench Town is the best, so I want to go there where the revellers is. I know these guys and they are very nice people to me. As you know, oppression cause a lot of badness: they just fight hard to survive, to live, y'know."

Trench Town, built on the site of a former sugar plantation, had once been a fashionable middle-class address. To the Ambassador's Theatre in its centre the hoi-polloi of Kingston in the late 1940s would flock to watch international stars like Louis Armstrong - they might find themselves seated next to such local luminaries as Noel Coward or the family of Sir Hugh Foot, the British Governor-General.

As the area was increasingly encroached upon by squatters' camps it went into economic decline. The middle class fled, with a measure of relief: Trench Town was in the hottest part of Kingston, almost untouched by the breezes from the Blue Mountains that wafted down to cool the city's more northerly, uptown reaches.

The squatters' camps, which had gradually been filling up west Kingston, had been built around the former Kingston refuse dump, from which the country folk and displaced city-dwellers who lived there would scavenge for whatever they could find. Following the devastating hurricane of 1951, which destroyed the shanty towns, the British colonial power replaced an area known as the Dungle with the low-rise housing scheme of Trench Town.

Is it true that Trench Town is named after the open sewer that ran through it?

This was desirable accommodation if your previous home had been a packing case. These 'government yards', as they became known around the world thanks to reggae mythology (as in the lines *"Do you remember when we used to sit/In a government yard in Trench Town"* from Bob Marley's 'No Woman No Cry'), were comprised of solidly constructed communal cooking facilities with a standpipe for water. Few were so ungrateful as to complain that Jamaica's colonial masters had seen fit to build Trench Town without any form of sewage system.

As a haven for outcasts, the area made an attractive home for unorthodox thinkers - especially members of the strange sect of Rastafarians who in the 1950s found themselves increasingly oppressed by the mystified, nervous authorities. It became the domicile of such notables as Mortimer Planner, who would lead Haile Selassie down the steps of his plane when it landed in

Kingston in 1966; of Joe Higgs, one half of the successful Higgs and Wilson singing duo, who would become a musical mentor to a young neighbourhood group called the Wailers; and of Alton Ellis, later one of Jamaica's most mellifluously beautiful - and, during the 1960s, most successful - vocalists, who moved to the area as soon as the first stage of the building of the government yards had been completed.

Ellis recalled Trench Town in the 1950s as a "peaceful, loving place". "When I went there," said the singer, "it was a new scheme, government-built for poor people." Each apartment within the individual complexes had two bedrooms; in the communal yard would be four toilets and bathrooms, by each gate was planted a mango or pawpaw tree. "But even though the place was nice, the poverty still existed. The poverty was so strong that you know what that lead to."

"No man, them call it that because of Mr Trench, the builder." FATHER BOBBY WILMOTT

Indisputably the number one rocksteady and reggae vocal trio, the Heptones are the archetype for all Jamaican three-piece male harmony groups. Comprised of Leroy Sibbles, Barry Llewellyn and Earl Morgan, the Heptones worked at Studio One for five years. After their first hit, the somewhat lewd 'Fattie Fattie' they proved unstoppable. Sibbles' voice had superb control, although the other two group members would from time to time also take the lead part. The group's first two albums for Studio One, The Heptones and Heptones on Top, are records that can hardly be equalled. Sibbles had also worked at Studio One as arranger, bassist and part-time A&R man; so when there was an acrimonious split with Coxsone Dodd, it was he who especially felt it. The same line-up recorded the Party Time album for Scratch Perry, which came out on Island overseas. When the record failed to sell significantly, Sibbles left the group for a solo career, basing himself in Canada. He was replaced by Naggo Morris, but this new line-up lacked the magic of the original.

In his inner city constituency of Tivoli Gardens in downtown Kingston, Edward Seaga signed up the locally-based Tivoli Gang to carry out a role not dissimilar to that they enacted for sound systems - except that the opposition now to be mashed up was the rival political party, the People's National Party (PNP), and its members.

The PNP, led by Michael Manley, immediately responded to this dangerous threat to the balance of power: a gang of Duke Reid followers known as the Spanglers, from the PNP stronghold of Back O' Wall, were taken on as equalisers. Violence escalated, with guns being employed on a wide scale in Jamaica for the first time, panicking the populace: in the build-up to elections in 1966 a state of emergency was called. Here lie the origins of the badmen drug posses that came to rule in the 1980s, not only in Jamaica but also in the USA. More immediately, it gave a huge international hit record to Desmond Dekker, whose '007 (Shanty Town)' for Leslie Kong's Beverley's label gave expression to these terrible troubles: "*Dem a-loot, dem a-shoot, dem a-burn down shanty town*". Whether these lyrics had any real meaning for the record-buyers in the UK and USA who made the record rocksteady's first international hit remains debatable.

Songs about rude boys had first surfaced in 1963, with a Duke Reid instrumental entitled 'Rude Boy'. But it was the Wailers, in their first recording 'Simmer Down', who lyrically linked the music directly with the rude boys. The song was hardly a musical encouragement of the activities of the rude boys; rather, it warned the rudies to cool it ("*Simmer down/Control your temper/Simmer down/'Cause the battle will be hotter*"). Released just before Christmas 1963, this ska record was number one in the Jamaican charts by the beginning of February 1964. The tune's subject of teenage crime established the Wailers as the musical front of the rude boys, who hardly seemed to notice the implied criticisms of their activities in the song. 'Simmer Down''s subject matter made the Wailers stand out amongst their contemporaries: up until then no one in Jamaican music had been expressing ghetto thinking. The Wailers recorded two more songs that were specifically about this youth

What did you think to the young Bob Marley?

Bob came with his group the Wailers. And they had this tune, and you noticed there was no ending to this tune, the way it was being put together. So I had to play little beginnings and endings to it, and I feel it came out okay. Well, a lot of people liked it. That was how he got his first hit, 'It Hurts To Be Alone'. Then I did 'I'm Still Waiting' and 'Simmer Down' and things like that. I could see that Bob was going to be some great guy, because he was so attentive to what was going on. I saw this man is a perfectionist. Everything has to be the way he wants it. So I would see this young guy is going to be a great man.

ERNEST RANGLIN

Left: The Wailers line-up of Bunny Livingston, Bob Marley and Peter Tosh (left to right) were willing participants in Coxsone Dodd's efforts to bring a Motown-like code of appearance to the stars of Studio One.

tribe: a 1965 tune that, like the earlier Duke Reid instrumental, was actually called 'Rude Boy'; and a stronger song, 'Jailhouse', in 1966, which included the lyrics *"The baton sticks get shorter/Rudie get taller"*.

Another outfit that recorded rude boy songs for Coxsone was the Clarendonians. With their songs 'Rudie Gone A Jail' and 'Rudie Bam Bam', they had more success than the Wailers did with their last two rude boy records. Initially comprised of the duo of Fitzroy 'Ernest' Wilson and Peter Austin, who were in their very early teens, they then brought their average age down even lower with the addition of the seven-year-old Freddie McGregor.

The Clarendonians' records were specifically in the

rocksteady mould. Although it only lasted for a brief period, the cool soulful feel of rocksteady was colossally influential. The piano and brass, so dominant in ska, became a supportive sound in rocksteady; the rhythmic focus was shifted onto the drums and the recent - certainly in Jamaica - innovation of the electric bass. This remained the dominant theme for subsequent Jamaican music; as rocksteady developed, bass patterns became more complicated, and percussion more complex.

Several records vied for the title of the first rocksteady tune, amongst them Roy Shirley's 'Hold Them', Derrick Morgan's 'Tougher Than Tough', and Alton Ellis's 'Girl I've Got A Date'.

A 'foundation' member of the Jamaican music scene, Derrick Morgan was a serious player in events surrounding the birth of the island's record industry.

You started out making records for Duke Reid's sound?

Oh yes. That's how we fall out.

Because he was playing the record 'Lover Boy' on the sound. I wrote it and called it 'Lover Boy', but it got a name for itself as 'S-Corner Rock'. That was a corner where Edwards Sound used to play, and he have an acetate of it that he play on that corner. So I heard of this man called Lickle Wonder. He was doing recording for himself. I went to him and sing him 'S-Corner Rock', and he was surprised and want to do a song with me. So what I did, I sang the song 'Hey You Fat Man' for him.

Anyhow, after I do 'Fat Man', he release it, a number one seller. Then Duke Reid heard of it and he sent some badmen. And they said "The Duke want to see you". And I say, "Why?", and they say, "Because you sing for another man and you shouldn't do that: you are contracted to Duke". I didn't feel good that I was afraid of those men. Anyhow, I went.

Duke told you not to go and sing for anyone else: did anyone approach you?

Yes. Way up on Orange Street, I met

this guy called Prince Buster and he say that him get a loan and have some money and would like to do some recording with me. I was with Monty Morris [Eric Morris] and I say, "Alright, boss", and "Where yuh get the name Prince? Yuh father is not a king". So 'im have a session two days later, and I do a song called 'Shake A Leg' and Monty Morris do 'Humpty Dumpty' - Buster's first session. He do about 13 songs that day; they was all hit songs.

When did you leave Prince Buster?

Prince get jealous in 1962, when I made

'Forward March' for Beverley's. Prince says, "I don't like that because you take my song and give it to Beverley's". I say, "What song?" He say the horn solo sound very like one on a tune called 'They Got To Come'. And for that he write a song about me called 'Blackhead Chinaman'. I used to do auditions for Beverley's, play a little keyboards. And I say, "If Prince say I am a Blackhead Chinaman, he can walk the blazing fire". And I write the song 'Blazing Fire'. And that outsell him.

How did you meet Bob Marley?

About 1962 I used to drink liquor at a bar on Charles Street at Spanish

Town Road - is Tivoli now, but it used to be Back O' Wall. And I have a girlfriend called Pat Stewart: we used to meet there and drink. She introduced Bob to me as a good singer, and he have a song. I say, "Why don't you come by Beverley's and we'll listen to you?" About two or three days later, he came there with Jimmy Cliff, and we listened to his song 'Judge Not'.

At the same time I was leaving for England. Prince Buster have a manager called Shalett who used to run Blue Beat: he wanted me to come up on a contract. He gave me £900 to come to England to sign for him - a lot of money in those days. I never sign no papers with Beverley's, and Leslie Kong just wanted me to keep giving him hit songs. So I signed for Shallett, and me and Buster go. When Leslie find he can't stop me, he decide to put on three farewell shows.

All the shows was nice, but this is where Bob get his first show. In May Pen, what he did was he danced - he used to be a good dancer. He danced all the while that I was singing. And he was very tired. I took him backstage and said, "You, that not the way yuh must do it - yuh mus' sing and when the solo come yuh must dance. But if you do it all the way through, you gwan be dead - too much energy you using". So the first line him sing, him just do the actions when he sing, but not dance. But they boo him the first song - I was even wondering if it was because he was doing it my way. But then him go straight on to *'Judge not, before you judge yourself'*. And the audience believe he was singing it because of them. And he steal the show from us with that song. It is my pleasure to say, "Yes, I was the first man to audition Bob".

How did you get involved in rocksteady?

After I come back from England,

Beverley's took me back again. And the first thing I gave them was 'Tougher Than Tough'. Then I start giving him songs like 'Greedy Girl' and 'Woman No Grumble'. Beverley's glad to have him back in his camp. And I was hitting rocksteady. For the 'Tougher Than Tough' session, this gentleman called Lynn Taitt came from Trinidad to play organ for Byron Lee. And they didn't want him to play, so he take up his guitar and Beverley's used him on that session. Lynn Taitt started playing that kind of rhythm on his guitar bass-strings different from the straight bass, breaking it up.

Derrick Morgan, who was born in March 1940, began his career by imitating Little Richard at a talent concert at the age of 15, when he beat off Owen Gray, Jackie Edwards, Eric Morris and Hortense Ellis (the sister of Alton Ellis): at first Morgan toured as 'Little Richie'. He first came to recording prominence in 1959, when he recorded 'Lover Boy' for Duke Reid. When he made records for another producer, Reid threatened him, and Morgan agreed to make a series of duets with the female singer Patsy. He then moved to work with Prince Buster, on 'Shake A Leg' and 'Lulu'. But his greatest work came when he upped producers yet again, this time working with Leslie Kong: at one time the Jamaican Top Ten had seven records by Morgan in it, all on Kong's Beverley's label, including the classic 'Be Still' and a huge smash, 'Housewife's Choice'. Morgan also introduced Bob Marley to Kong. Falling out with Buster because of his work with Kong, Morgan recorded 'Blazing Fire', a boasting battle anthem directed at the Prince. Later Morgan made rocksteady masterpieces of sweet simplicity like 'You Never Miss The Water', and moving to the UK, became a favourite with mod and skinhead audiences.

Forward MARCH!

SIDE 1
1 Forward March
2 The Hop
3 Look before You Leap
4 Don't You be a Fool
5 It's True My Darling
6 Housewife's Choice

SIDE 2
1 The Blazing Fire
2 I've found a Queen
3 Teach My Baby
4 Angel with Blue Eyes
5 Last Chance
6 Don't You Worry

DERRICK MORGAN

And that's
how the rocksteady really started.
They give it a name rocksteady from how
the people really dance to the song.
Then everybody started copying the style.

In June 1964 Millicent
'Millie' Small - born in
Clarendon, Jamaica in
1942 - went to London,
where Chris Blackwell
had set up Island
Records, a small company
initially targeted at his
fellow expatriate Jamaicans. Millie had come to Blackwell's attention after scoring hits
as part of the Roy and Millie duo - as well as working with Roy Panton, she had also
recorded with Jackie Edwards and Derrick Morgan. In London Blackwell enlisted the
aid of master guitarist Ernest Ranglin and his arranging skills, and put Millie in the
studio to record a version of Barbie Gaye's 1957 R'n'B hit 'My Boy Lollipop'. Aware of
the record's pop possibilities, Blackwell licensed the disc to the Fontana label: the
result was an international hit that sold seven million copies. Despite the pop feel of
the record, however, Ranglin's ska arrangement slots the tune into a style that does
not let it stand at all out of place when played next to such luminaries as the Skatalites.
Below: 'My Boy Lollipop' was also released on the Beverley's label, run by Leslie Kong
(in middle of the 45). Kong was an influential producer, recording Bob Marley's early
releases 'Judge Not' and 'One Cup Of Coffee', and working with most of Jamaica's
leading musicians - including Desmond
Dekker ('007' and 'The Israelites')
and the Maytals ('54-46
That's My Number' and
'Monkey Man') - before
his death from a heart
attack in 1971.

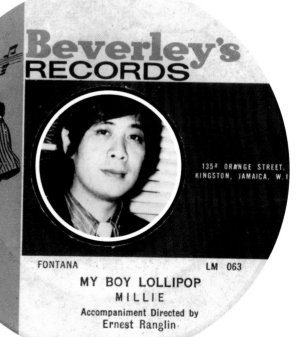

Not everyone in the artistic community perceived the rudies as a force to be encouraged.

For Duke Reid the great Alton Ellis recorded five anti-rude boy singles, among them the classic 'Cry Tough', which - in collusion with the gruff-voiced Lloyd Charmers - clearly stated his view: *"How can a man be tough/Tougher than the world/ For if a man is rough/He's against the world"*. Not only did Ellis consistently take an anti-Rude Boy stance, but he actively blamed the Wailers for encouraging their nefarious activities.

Alton Ellis was one of Jamaica's most successful and influential vocalists, especially during the rocksteady era when he recorded copiously for Duke Reid. A strong songwriter, Ellis had a talent for taking American soul tunes and rendering them specifically Jamaican. An early inhabitant of the new housing scheme built in Trench Town, Ellis first recorded in the late 1950s with singer Eddy Perkins as one-half of the duo Alton and Eddy - 'Muriel' was a huge hit for them. Working as Alton Ellis and the Flames, it was a tribute to his colossal talent that he managed the delicate tightrope walk of working for both Coxsone Dodd and Duke Reid. Rocksteady amply suited him: it gave singers more space in which to stretch out, as on his big hit simply titled 'Rock Steady' and as heard to the fullest on the Treasure Isle rocksteady album, *Mr Soul Of Jamaica*. He now performs and records infrequently, but remains one of the all-time greats of Jamaican music.

Alton Ellis

The Alton Ellis track 'Girl I've Got A Date' was produced by Duke Reid. Whatever the veracity behind the various claims for having had the first rocksteady disc out of the traps, one fact was certain: Duke Reid seized the rocksteady moment with a sure grip that eluded his great rival Coxsone Dodd.

Although Coxsone was to enjoy success with the Wailers' tune 'Rocking Steady' - which contained the Bob Marley lyrics *"When first I heard rocksteady/it thrilled me to the bone"* - his studio had momentarily lost momentum. (Besides, the Wailers were about to quit the Coxsone stable for good.)

Duke Reid's Treasure Isle studio, a wood-panelled structure located above his liquor store at 33 Bond Street, won its spurs as the finest rocksteady tunes emerged from it, classics like 'Happy Go Lucky Girl' by the Paragons, Dobby Dobson's magnificent 'Loving Pauper', Phyllis Dillon's heartfelt 'Don't Stay Away', and many, many fabulous tunes from the great Alton Ellis, including a song actually called 'Rock Steady' (*"You've got to do this new dance/If you are ready"*).

Rocksteady was really a Jamaican counterpart of contemporary American soul music: for example, The Techniques' excellent 'Queen Majesty', another Duke Reid record, was modelled on 'Minstrel And Queen' by the Impressions, a major influence on many Jamaican acts. When 'Ruddy' Redwood, who ran the most prominent sound system in Spanish Town, remixed Treasure Isle instrumentals, they led to the dub of the 1970s; and it was over Treasure Isle rocksteady tunes that U-Roy first deejayed.

The sense of space in rocksteady opened the possibilities for more complex or subtle arrangements. Tommy McCook and the Supersonics were fundamental in shaping the sound and style of this new Jamaican music - McCook was employed exclusively by Duke Reid. In the Jamaican musical world no man was an island, however, and artists constantly interweaved. Lynn Taitt, a Trinidadian guitarist who arranged almost all the best known early examples of rocksteady, was one of the genre's most significant musicians: he would play the bass strings of his guitar in unison with the bassist.

A musician who had played with the Skatalites, his group Lynn Taitt and the Jets were the principal rocksteady session group on the island outside of Treasure Isle - most of them also performing as members of Tommy McCook and the Supersonics. For Winston 'Merritone' Blake, Taitt and the Jets played on the great 'Take It Easy' by Hopeton Lewis, himself a member of the group: one of the first rocksteady records, it was a huge hit, selling 10,000 copies in one weekend after it had been aired on Charlie Babcock's radio show; they also played on countless hits for Duke Reid, Mrs Sonia Pottinger, Bunny Lee, WIRL, Federal and Derrick Harriott, whose 'The Loser' is another crucial rocksteady tune.

Like most Jamaican session musicians, the Jets' work rate was prodigious, often playing on numerous sessions in one day. Amongst these players were vocalist Hopeton Lewis, horn-player Headley Bennett, pianist Gladstone Anderson, guitarist Hux Brown and Winston Wright, master of the Hammond organ. (Later Taitt played on Johnny Nash's 'Cupid' and 'Hold Me Tight', which made the British pop charts.)

The successful adaptation to the new style by the likes of the Maytals and Desmond Dekker and the Aces inspired the formation of new trios and quartets, and soon Jamaica was awash with new harmony groups: for example, the

Heptones, the Gaylads, the Ethiopians, the Melodians, and the Techniques. Within a year, however, a trio of producers - Bunny Lee, Lee 'Scratch' Perry and Osbourne 'King Tubby' Ruddock - were to have brought about a third change, into reggae music.

Out of Africa came the sound of reggae. Once I sat in a lean-to on the edge of the Sahara desert in Senegal: as a host of musicians entered it to perform praise songs for the great local musician Baaba Maal, on such beautiful native instruments as koras and hoddus, I marvelled as I heard what was quite clearly the rhythm of reggae. When Jimmy Cliff went to Senegal he had the same experience. "Now I know where reggae came from," he said.

Although the title of the Maytals' August 1968 release 'Do The Reggay' has given it some credibility as the first reggae record, that year had already seen several other tunes using a faster rhythm than rocksteady. From Coxsone Dodd had come Larry Marshall's 'Nanny Goat', set to Jackie Mittoo's shuffling organ sound. And Harry 'J' Johnson had released 'No More Heartaches' by the Beltones. Both these records were recorded at Studio One - at first Harry J would lease time from Coxsone.

There were other contenders for the title of first reggae record. Because of his guitar sound Alva Lewis claims it for the tune 'Bangarang', a Bunny Lee production recorded in

Born in Cuba in 1927, Laurel Aitken recorded 'Boogie In My Bones' in 1958 for the new Island label started in Jamaica by Chris Blackwell. The record was an early example of what became known as Jamaican 'blues' music - localised variants on the shuffle-boogie R'n'B records coming out of New Orleans, which were the precursors of ska. When ska itself hit, Aitken enjoyed a string of successes, both in Jamaica and England. Moving to the UK, he based himself first in London and then in Leicester, recording scores of songs for Emile Shalett's Blue Beat label, Graeme Goodall's Rio Records, and the Palmer brothers' Nu Beat. Aitken's fan base amongst initially mods and subsequently skinheads assured him of a second crack at his career in the late 1970s with the 2-Tone ska revival.

1969 at Treasure Isle and credited to Stranger Cole and Lester Sterling: the song was a development of 'Bongo Chant', a British bop tune from a decade before by Kenny Graham and the Afro-Cubists. Producer Bunny 'Striker' Lee also argues that 'Bangarang' was the first reggae song, but not, he insisted, because of the guitar sound but because of novice organ player Glen Adams' riffs - Striker was adamant that it was a kind of slurred organ sound, as specialised in by Jackie Mittoo (who was also an arranger and A&R man for Coxsone) that defined the first reggae records.

It is certainly notable how many early reggae records are dominated by an organ sound - for example, 'The Liquidator' by Harry J Allstars, featuring the Hammond organ of Winston Wright, a Top Ten hit in the UK the same year.

The year of 1968 had begun, meanwhile, with the faster rhythm of Lynford Anderson's 'Pop A Top'. What all these records really showed was that Jamaican music was opening up, becoming multi-faceted. Not all the new songs had a faster rhythm than rocksteady; some were

actually slower. But a characteristic of all of these songs in what was clearly a new, broadly expansive genre was that they were rougher in sound, and dominated by the bass even more than Jamaican music was already.

Guitarist Ernest Ranglin, meanwhile, claims it was he, Lee 'Scratch' Perry and Clancy Eccles who came up with the style at a joint session; Scratch and Eccles were the producers and Ranglin was the arranger on a Clancy tune called 'Feel The Rhythm'.

By the summer of 1968 Lynford Anderson collaborated with Lee Perry on 'People Funny Boy', a tune whose fast rhythm had a persistent guitar riff, one of the defining characteristics of reggae, a word that has over time become a generic term for Jamaican music. The music of 'People Funny Boy' was so extreme and peculiar that it went further than tunes like 'Nanny Goat' and 'No More Heartaches'. In some ways, however, it was such a unique record that, with its pronounced beat and African feel, especially that of its percussion, it almost stands alone, especially in comparison with the more measured contributions of Toots Hibbert and the Maytals.

Toots and the Maytals recorded 'Do The Reggay' in 1968 - for once the words 'seminal recording' are valid.

In 1961 Frederick 'Toots' Hibbert, a native of May Pen, a town in the middle of the island, joined forces with Nathaniel 'Jerry' Matthias and Henry 'Raleigh' Gordon as The Maytals. Soon they were recording for Coxsone Dodd. Working with the new ska beat played by the musicians who would later comprise the Skatalites, the Maytals matched it to the Baptist preacher feel of their harmonies. After recording such titles as 'Hallelujah', 'Fever' and their classic '6&7 Books Of Moses', they had become the biggest group in Jamaica. As Coxsone was only paying them £3 a side, they departed to work with Prince Buster. Soon, however, The Maytals were recording with Byron Lee, for whom they made another classic, 'Daddy'. But their enormous status on the island was dented in 1966 when Toots was busted for possession of marijuana. He served two years in prison, on his release putting out '54-46 That's My Number' for Leslie Kong, another timeless hit that pre-dated the new sound of reggae. Other renowned new songs from the group were 'Do The Reggay', 'Monkey Man' and 'Pressure Drop'. Signed to Island Records, Toots and the Maytals produced a number of archetypal records that acted to introduce reggae to a mainstream audience in the 1970s, notably the *Funky Kingston* and *Reggae Got Soul* LP sets. To this day, the group perform live, with Toots himself considered a kind of Otis Redding of reggae.

When did you first discover your singing voice?

It was way back. I used to go to church with my parents, a kind of clap-and-church, where they used to have concerts. I was about twelve. Every time I sound, people would make a lot of noise - clap and joyful. At singing class everybody lift me up, so I come up in a churchical order. So that where the talent come from - most of my songs are coming from the church. Not political really, though sometimes people may find it that way too.

Where were you brought up in Jamaica?

In May Pen. I come to Kingston when I was about 13. When I grow up I find this church called Coptic. And that's where I was for a long, long time, and stopped singing, just to know about the truth of Rastafari. I just heard of the Coptic church, and went up there in the hills above Montego Bay and saw them and talk and they know that I was one of them prophet. I know there are certain things you have to do in this world, and once you do it, you know you are one of them.

When did you start your professional career?

I first came from the country after people tell me I can sing, and I was searching out this singing business in Trench Town. King Edwards was a very great man, and he just say, "I like the way you sing, mon". I sang a song called 'Rosemarie', one of my first compositions. It was a dub plate. So he was a good man right there. Start me off.

I think it's Coxsone I go to next - Mr Dodd. He taught me from there. We cut a whole lot of songs, didn't care about the money. He always say, "Let's do it". And he always set the rhythm. It was good.

Would you sing the songs to the musicians?

In those days there was a lot of musicians, but the main musicians was Skatalites and Count Ossie and all those great men. When I came from country, I first met Count Ossie. I met Jah Jerry - he took me round to Count Ossie. And go to the studio and sing to them one time. Some time you just go in and sing it in the studio and record it one time: man just get the key and that's it.

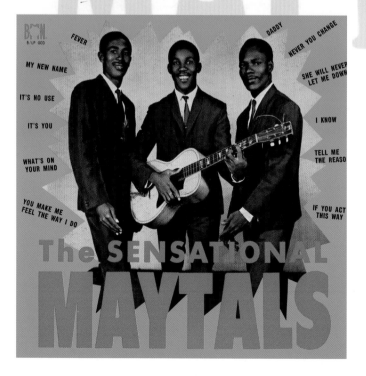

Toots' former career as a barber probably ensured he would never grow dreadlocks. Although one of reggae's international pioneers, the fact that his espousal of Rastafari was only internal went against him during the late 1970s.

How did the Maytals come together?

In Trench Town I used to be a barber.

I learned the trade in a barber's shop, and I make my little four-string guitar and I have it all the while and people listen to it in the barber's shop. So one day Raleigh [Henry Gordon] come down and listen to me and after a while someone come for a trim.

And Raleigh say to me, "Where yuh come from?" I say, "I come from country: I'm a country boy, sir". He say, "No man, you don't have to call me sir, man. I like what you do. Teach me how to sing".

So I meet Jerry [Nathaniel Matthias] the next day, and they take me up the house, and we sit under a ginep tree. And everybody just start to sing. And them say, "Yeah, man!" Them want to join me. So I start to teach them. I teach them harmony. I teach them how to write song. And they teach me how to grow up.

Toots Hibbert and the Maytals' *Reggae Got Soul* album, the biggest seller of their career, was a UK chart hit in 1976. Four years later, their stage performance was captured on the *Toots Live* album which was on sale in the shops 24 hours after being recorded at London's Hammersmith Palais on 29th September 1980. Although the speed with which the album had been mixed, mastered and pressed was clearly a marketing gimmick, the power and (not surprisingly) the spontaneity of the live record was unsurpassed.

What did ska mean to you?

Ska means very great things. Up music

that really lifts up artists and Jamaica because it is kind of new. After shuffle-boogie, which is like R'n'B, and ska works with those kind of beats too. Ska is our first music, and we cannot forget it.

You were the first man to use the word 'reggae' in a song title.

Even before that rocksteady was just there, just very near, just a different drum beat.

In Trench Town one day myself, Jerry and Raleigh was just sitting down rehearsing. Another guy was next door talking to a girl, and the girl was a nice girl but - just for argument's sake - we use the word 'streggae' about her, just a something going on: if something's going on with someone, and you don't want to talk to him, you'll just say, "He's streggae". So we say, "Let's do the reggae, Raleigh. Let's do the reggae, man". That's how the word just come. I didn't know it was going to be like that. I saw it in the *Guinness Book Of Records*. I think it was a good thing I did that: I think it was the power of the most high.

Everyone who listen to my song

after that, they tell me that they feel a different spirit, that I revive their spirit. If they was down the music just lift them up. So I was really proud of that, and it wasn't me by myself - it was the power of the most high. I say, up until now, if I'm doing something I have to do it with a certain spirit, to make sure the Father appreciate it. He give me the talent, really.

Where did the name 'Maytals' come from?

So after singing with Coxsone, we

sing a few songs for Prince Buster, also for Pottinger and for Duke Reid. We don't get no money really. In those days we get a pound or two pounds. Maybe five pounds. And we share it the three of us. And it go on like that for a long time. Until we were singing for Coxsone and go [kisses teeth]: "Want a singing name, y'know". And everybody say different names. And get up to go, and just say, "Maytal: it love mi a deal with". Maytal - it a word like 'ital' [pure]. So 'Maytals' just come like that, just like I say 'reggae'. The name just carry on from that time to this time. Stick together in one love. Anything wrong we just forgive it: maytal, don't carry feelings - if wi hurt, wi just talk about it. Maytal, like maytal food: just plant it, don't put any fertiliser. Don't hurt people. Maytal, like ital, so you don't take anything if it's not right.

Everyone who is Rasta have to be maytal, to do the right thing. Treat everyone

good when you can. Rasta means God, the prophet of God. Maytal means you have to be like a lamb, slow to anger. You always have that light shining.

When I was a little baby, people called me Toots. Nobody knowed that name. Until this man Charlie Babcock interviewed me, and the name just come out. And when they pinned that ganja charge on me - even the guy who did it told me that someone told him to do it: I'd just won the song festival, y'know.

But I wrote a song about the ganja pinning, and it hurt many people more than me. And plenty people didn't even realise what they heard. Things that you do well let you know you're a prophet of God. And things you do badly let you know you're maybe a prophet of the devil.

Little Richard used to say, "Rhythm'n'blues had a baby and they called it rock'n'roll". I say also that **rhythm'n'blues had a baby and they called it reggae.** WINSTON 'MERRITONE' BLAKE

"Yeah, reggae is music I tell you that I love right off. **It's got a good feel to it. Especially in Jamaica it somehow relates to the people.** This was one of the most important things about it. Most of the world has started singing the reggae and the words have a spiritual influence. I always feel good about reggae like rock steady and ska. **I look at them as little children of ska."**

PRINCE BUSTER

As the new reggae music began to develop, a leading role was being played by Lee 'Scratch' Perry. Starting out as a sound system box lifter, Perry had supervised auditions and record distribution for Studio One, but felt exploited. In 1967, accordingly, he had released 'The Upsetter', a rocksteady tune aimed at Coxsone Dodd, condemning

record, and as a result bought his first car, a Jaguar. Joe Gibbs even replied to 'People Funny Boy' with an answer song called 'People Grudgeful', employing the sound of a whining puppy to sneer at Scratch.

"If not the first reggae record," said David Katz, Scratch Perry's official biographer, "'People Funny Boy' is the most significant of those early records, with the most pronounced beat. In a way, its uniqueness slightly

Dodd
for his 'gravelicious'
[greedy] nature, and for not
treating him well 'cashically'. The ubiquitous
Lynn Taitt had played double-tracked guitar on the record,
which formed part of the Jamaican musical tradition of
airing feuds publicly on vinyl.

works
against it, because
subsequent musicians have drawn on
tunes like 'Nanny Goat' and 'No More Heartaches'
much more."

The commentary on 'People Funny Boy', his next vinyl-based attack, was far more revolutionary. 'The Upsetter', as Perry was by now also known, had recorded some tunes for up-and-coming producer Joe Gibbs; 'People Funny Boy' was an attack on Gibbs in which Scratch asserted that the producer had stolen his talents to become rich and left Lee Perry starving. "*Why, why, people funny bwai,*" he complained, his vocals underpinned by Winston Wright's extraordinary organ melody, against a musical background that sounded as though it had come from the heart of Africa. Scratch sold 60,000 copies of the

'People Funny Boy' was a big hit amongst Britain's Jamaican community. And soon Scratch had an instrumental hit, credited to the Upsetters, that crossed over into the UK pop charts. 'Return Of Django', its title inspired by the Sergio Corbucci spaghetti western, was a number five hit in October 1969; it featured the memorable sound of tenor-sax master Val Bennett. In the United Kingdom, the audience for such fast, jerky instrumental records as the Harry J Allstars' 'Liquidator', the number one UK smash of Dave and Ansell Collins' 'Double Barrel' (which combined an organ sound with early Jamaican deejaying) and 'Return Of Django' was largely made up of skinheads - around 1966 mods, the early white torchbearers for ska, had mutated into either hippies or skinheads.

As youth culture changed in the UK, so one event in

followers, Haile Selassie at first remained on the plane, until he was led down its steps by Mortimer Planner (aka Planno), a Rastafarian elder from Trench Town who had personally travelled to Ethiopia.

His Majesty had stopped in Jamaica on his way to the island of Trinidad. This official visit by a head of state caused considerable consternation for the deeply conservative administrators of the recently independent

John Holt (far left) is one of the all-time greats of Jamaican music, whether as a member of the Paragons, as a performer of lush soul reggae on his *1,000 Volts Of Holt* LP series, or recording such reality songs as 'Police In Helicopter' with Junjo Lawes. Scratch Perry's song and album titles (centre) clearly show the influence of spaghetti Westerns. And trombonist Rico Rodriguez (right) is part of the bedrock of Jamaican music - in the early 1960s he was a mainstay of ska sessions; moving to London he played with Georgie Fame; and in 1976 he released *Man From Wareika*, his masterly album of jazz-reggae.

Jamaica changed the spirit of Jamaica irrevocably. On 21st April 1966 a plane bearing His Imperial Majesty Haile Selassie I arrowed down from the sky, guided down by a flock of seven white doves, breaking apart the 100% cloud cover to reveal blue sky and sunshine. Norman Manley Airport, situated on the same narrow isthmus as Port Royal, the former pirate capital of the island, was over-run with Rastafarians, who had trekked from all over the island to greet the arrival of His Majesty, who many revered as God himself. Even the airport runway was surrounded by dreads as Haile Selassie's plane pulled to a halt on the tarmac. Overwhelmed by the sight of so many

island: on the one hand it was clearly an honour that this African ruler should visit the island; on the other, there was the troubling question of the loyalty expressed to him by Jamaica's Rastafarians, who were essentially unmentionables. Moreover, the visit served as a catalyst for conversion to the faith of Rastafari for many islanders, including Rita Marley. In the absence of her husband Bob in the United States, she had made her way over to the Windward Road, which leads in from the airport, hoping to catch a glimpse of the Ethiopian Emperor.

As the Daimler limousine drew parallel with her, Rita's thoughts were not positive. "How is it they are saying that this man is so great," she wondered, "when he looks so short, with his army hat over his head in such a way I can't even see his eyes?"

"Then I said to myself, 'What am I even thinking about? Jesus is a spirit.'" At that exact moment Haile Selassie raised his face: he looked directly into Rita's eyes

and waved. "And I looked into his hand and there was the nail-print. It was a mark, and I could only identify that mark with the scriptures of history, saying, 'When you see him, you will know him by the nail-print in his hands'. So when I saw this, I said to myself that this could be true, this could be the man of whom it was said, 'Before the year 2000 Christ will be a man walking on this earth.'"

Rita told her husband of her experience, and Bob Marley's life was changed forever. As was that of many, many inhabitants of the island of Jamaica. Rastafari had always had an important place in Jamaican music. Studio One, for example, was favoured by many musicians on account of Coxsone Dodd's casting a blind eye to the smoking of ganja, considered as a sacrament by many Rastafarians. (Duke Reid, the former policeman, would have no truck with consumption of herb at Treasure Isle.) From now on, however, belief in this apparently curious faith was to take a quantum leap, developing until it became to a large extent the principal philosophical motor of the music.

Yet this was still below wraps. The success of 'People Funny Boy' had pushed the reputation of Lee 'Scratch' Perry - who would become one of the principal musical proselytisers of Rastafari - up to the point where he could strike a licensing deal for his Upsetter Records in the United Kingdom with the Trojan label, which had originally been set up to release Duke Reid's Treasure Isle material in Britain.

Now that the new Jamaican music of reggae was growing in popularity there, Scratch inked a deal for Upsetter material with Trojan. His tune 'Tighten Up' was as popular as 'People Funny Boy' had been; its title gave the name to a series of budget-priced compilation records on Trojan that deservedly came to be regarded as classics. Unusually for British records, the sleeve credits listed the producer's name after the title, rather than giving the composer's credit.

Three of the twelve cuts on the first *Tighten Up* album, released in 1969, bore the credit 'Prod. Lee Perry' - 'Tighten Up' by the Untouchables, 'Spanish Harlem' by Val Bennett, and 'Place In The Sun' by David Isaacs. Duke Reid had two tunes on the album, both by Joya Landis: 'Kansas City' and 'Angel Of The Morning'. The same year Scratch Perry was asked to set up his own Upsetter label through Trojan.

The years 1969 and 1970, which coincided with the peak of skinhead power, saw a virtual deluge of Jamaican hits in the UK: Desmond Dekker had a number one with 'Israelites', whilst 'It Mek' also made the Top Ten. Jimmy Cliff hit the Top Ten with 'Wonderful World, Beautiful People' and 'Wide World'. Bob Andy and Marcia Griffiths entered the Top Five with a crisp Harry J production of Nina Simone's 'Young, Gifted And Black', and Max Romeo courted controversy with the extremely catchy 'Wet Dream'. Thanks to a BBC-imposed ban on airplay, this Bunny Lee-produced tune skirted the UK Top Ten for much of the summer of 1969, selling over a quarter of a million copies. and introducing an atmosphere of

Left: Jackie Edwards was a constant element of Jamaican music and one of its great ambassadors throughout the 1960s, able to record anything from ska to rocksteady to reggae as required. After writing and performing 'Your Eyes Are Dreaming', and 'Tell Me Darling' for Chris Blackwell in 1959, Edwards recorded hundreds of songs. Moving to the UK with Blackwell in 1962, he continued writing and recording. But his biggest successes came in 1966 when the Spencer Davis Group had two consecutive UK number one hits with songs he had written - 'Keep On Running' and 'Somebody Help Me'.

Right: Desmond Dekker was the first Jamaican singer to feature regularly in the overseas charts. With a Leslie Kong production, his first big hit '007 (Shanty Town)', in the new rocksteady vein, was the finest of all the songs celebrating the arrival of the rude boy. 'Israelites' was an even bigger record, the first truly international Jamaican hit, number nine in the USA in 1969, and a number one in the UK. With his backing group the Aces, Dekker enjoyed twenty number one hits in Jamaica during the mid to late-1960s. Moving to the UK, his fortunes became more erratic.

'slackness' - *"Lie down girl/Let me push it up, push it up"* ran one couplet. During this period Nicky Thomas, the Melodians, Boris Gardiner and the Pioneers also had UK chart hits.

By the beginning of the 1970s, the lyrical themes of reggae music were becoming more specific. 'Move Out A Babylon', proclaimed Johnnie Clarke. *"Curly locks/You know that I'm a dreadlocks,"* sang Junior Byles. It was clear that the apparently curious ideas expressed in the likes of Desmond Dekker's 'Israelites' and the Melodians' 'Rivers Of Babylon' (their version of Psalm 137 was a worldwide disco hit for Boney M in 1975) were hardly one-off eccentricities, but part of a universal current of thought.

And in 1972 *The Harder They Come*, Jamaica's first internationally successful film, ensured that in Britain reggae transcended its now diminishing skinhead audience. Perry Henzell's movie, which starred Jimmy Cliff in a classic tale of country-boy-goes-wrong-in-the-city, had one of the best soundtrack albums ever released.

As well as Jimmy Cliff's organ-based title song, it included - among other tracks - 'Pressure Drop' and 'Sweet And Dandy' by the Maytals, 'Johnny Too Bad' by the Slickers, Scotty's 'Draw Your Brakes' and two more songs from Jimmy Cliff: the beautiful 'Many Rivers To Cross' and 'You Can Get It If You Really Want' (the fact that the last song appeared on the record twice was an anomaly that no one seemed to comment on). As a primer for hip white kids wanting to find out about a new music it was invaluable, a *de rigueur* soundtrack to fashionable London dinner parties that ended with joints of Congolese bush. In the sexy rebel image sported by Jimmy Cliff in the movie, it looked as though Chris Blackwell, the white Jamaican who had founded Island Records, had found what he'd been seeking: a way to take reggae into the rock album market.

But then Jimmy Cliff told Blackwell that he was going to leave Island, criticising the amount of time the label boss had spent on rock music. To no avail a distressed Blackwell told him he believed his understanding of the rock market was crucial in trying to break reggae.

But a week later Bob Marley walked into the offices of Island Records. "He came in right at the time when in my head there was the idea that this rebel type of character could really emerge, and that I could break such an artist," said Blackwell. "I was dealing with rock music, which was really rebel music. I felt that would really be the way to break Jamaican music. But you needed somebody who could be that image. When Bob walked in he really was that image, the real one that Jimmy had created in the movie."

An excellent singer-songwriter, Jimmy Cliff was an international face of reggae music even before Bob Marley. In 1962, at the age of 15, he first emerged as a ska singer, having successes for Leslie Kong with 'King Of Kings' and 'Dearest Beverley'. Brought to the attention of Chris Blackwell, Cliff moved to London where he was groomed as an Island Records solo star. It was 1969 before he hit the UK pop charts, with his self-penned 'Wonderful World, Beautiful People', followed the next year by 'Vietnam'. Other hits included his cover of Cat Stevens' 'Wild World'. But Cliff's career took a quantum leap to iconic status when he starred as Ivan Rhygin in Perry Henzell's *The Harder They Come*. Although Chris Blackwell wanted to capitalise on this new recognition, Cliff left Island and signed with EMI. Although the quality of his work has never been in doubt, Jimmy Cliff never took full advantage of the break that *The Harder They Come* should have brought him. He remains, however, a huge star in Africa and South America.

In few places is the truth that necessity is the mother of invention more often borne out than in Jamaica. During the economic shortages which afflicted the island during the mid-1970s, might you, for example, have found your Ford Cortina in need of a new column gearstick?

DEEJAYS &

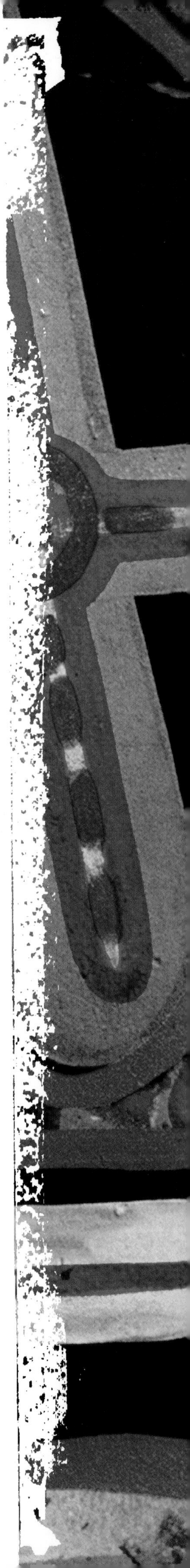

"No problem, suh," says the man at the garage: you come back and find you now have a floor-mounted gearstick taken from a Citroën. The existence of the sound system was perhaps the most important outcome of this roots version of post-modernism. For from this backyard culture also developed the era of the sound system deejay, first ushered in by Count

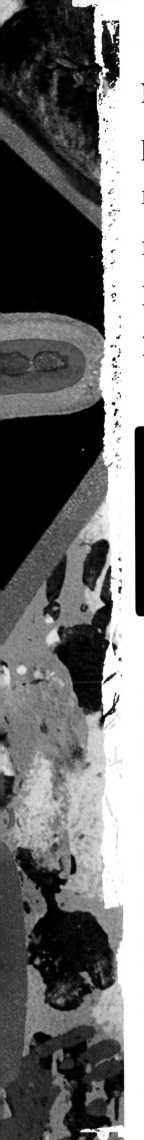

Machuki in the early 1950s and continued by his protégé King Stitt into the next decade. Few ska records featured deejays talking over them, and rocksteady seemed at first too languid. But as rocksteady gave way to reggae's faster style, the deejay had a new lease of life.

DUBMASTERS

However, at first 'toasting', as the art of deejaying was often known (in the same way that a maitre d' at a function would 'toast' guests), was considered by serious Jamaican musicians to be a lesser, street form - nothing more than a gimmick - even when Ewart Beckford, better known as U-Roy, became the first such artist to enjoy great record success.

Despite this view that deejaying was nothing but a nine-minute wonder, U-Roy, who used Duke Reid's existing rocksteady rhythms as the foundations for his vocals, became a local superstar through his recorded output: one week in 1970 he held the top three places in Jamaica's pop chart with 'Wake The Town', 'Rule The Nation' and 'Wear You To The Ball'. Such was his skill that when fear of electrocution caused sound systems to be switched off during Jamaica's regular tropical downpours, he would keep the dancers moving using only his unamplified vocals.

In 1961 U-Roy had started playing as a deejay with Doctor Dickies Dynamic sound system. "Dickie was just one of my friends," said Ewart 'U-Roy' Beckford. "He was a Chinese guy who have a business. And he have this sound system, so I used to go with them whenever I can, from when I was about 14. I didn't start holding a mike until a couple of years after that, because I was kind of shy. Then I start just taking up the mike and introducing the singers and say where the next dance gwan keep next week, and stuff like that."

It was the great Machuki who set U-Roy on his life course. "I used to love this deejay by the name of Count Machuki. He used to play a sound named Sir Coxsone's. I like his style. Because this man is a man who understand what he is talking about. He don't chat no stupidness. Relax when he deejay and he don't clash with the vocals. So I used to love that. That's really the man who inspire me in certain things."

U-Roy's career progression was like an archetypal deejay story - except that it was he who provided the original template. From Dickies Dynamic, U-Roy graduated in the mid-1960s to Sir George The Atomic, a sound based around Kingston's Maxfield Avenue. Then he moved to Coxsone's Downbeat number two 'set', at a time when King Stitt was the deejay-in-residence with Dodd's number one sound. Ranking sound operators would run more than one set, playing them in different venues: Stitt himself

had started off with number two Downbeat. In 1957 King Stitt, also known as 'The Ugly One', had been noticed by Count Machuki as he danced superlatively to the fast, tough style of R'n'B that Machuki would spin. With impeccable logic, Machuki told Stitt that if he was such a good dancer, he must also be a good deejay.

Accordingly, Stitt became number two deejay to Machuki, beginning to play on his own after about twelve weeks. When Machuki retired shortly afterwards, Stitt took up the baton, and it was Stitt who was the first deejay to have his verbal skills preserved on vinyl when in the late 1960s he made several hit records, such as 'Fire Corner' and 'Lee Van Cleef' (the 'Ugly One', in Sergio Leone's *The Good, The Bad And The Ugly*) - for producer Clancy Eccles.

Others deejays had followed Machuki and Stitt. Men like Sir Lord Comic, Cool Sticky and the sadly unrecorded Hopeton made their reputations stringing together rhymes and catch-phrases to introduce records, boost their sound system, make announcements and generally 'nice up the dance'. By the end of the 1950s the 'man-on-the-microphone' had become integral to the Jamaican sound system - the slick, jive-talking disc jockeys on US radio stations provided an inspiration.

Yet ska records featuring deejays were infrequent. Notable exceptions included Comic's 'Ska-ing West' and 'Great Wuga Wuga', and some great tunes featuring Sticky's extraordinary vocals ('Guns of Navarone' and 'Guns Fever', for example). The rocksteady years only provided a few sides for deejays to express themselves, but their time was coming, as the rocksteady beat was superseded by the faster tempo of reggae - an irony, subsequent things considered.

Following another brief spell with Sir George, U-Roy moved to King Tubby's Home-Town Hi-Fi, owned by a man who was to become another legend, Osbourne 'King Tubby' Ruddock. U-Roy was full of admiration for him. "Some people think themselves so great they think is they make this happen. Me, for example: people tell me,

Above: The very great U-Roy, without whom the history of late 20th-century music would have been very different - modestly, however, U-Roy passes the praise for the mass origin of deejay music to King Tubby.
Right: At Tapper Zukie's pressing plant.

"Tubby's was a man who have one of the greatest sounds. This man did his own sound system,

'You is the number one deejay, you is the best'. I am not the one who make me what I am - you get support both from the most high, and from the public. To make you be whatever you want to be. But this man Tubby was a genius. Him know the work."

By now U-Roy also was achieving great acclaim for the jive-talk toasts he would add over the dub plates that Tubby was beginning to turn out: he had learned the art of dropping out the vocals and re-mixing the instrumental tracks to literally resounding effect. "U-Roy had this echo thing," remembered Dennis Alcapone, by then operating his own El Paso sound system. "When introducing a music or advertising a dance, all his words would echo: it blow my mind. It was Tubby's that introduce reverb in

the dance. I never hear a thing like that, because reverb was mostly in the studios. But he had the reverb on the sound system and the echo. It was just brilliant. Tubby's have some steel speakers they used to put up in the trees, and when you listen to that sound system, especially at night when the wind is blowing the sound all over the place, it was wicked!"

Working with the dynamic presence of Lee 'Scratch' Perry, U-Roy began his recording career with a pair of tunes, 'Earth's Rightful Ruler' and 'OK Corral'; he also made the excellent 'Dynamic Fashion Way' for Keith Hudson. But these records failed to sell well.

U-Roy continued to deejay with Tubby. Then Duke Reid learned of his reputation, and asked to meet him.

he cut his own dub, so it hard to compete with him. He is ahead of you every time." U-ROY

According to John Holt, then the lead singer with the Paragons, the definitive Treasure Isle vocal harmony group, it was he who alerted Reid to this innovative new performer. "U-Roy was the deejay for Tubby's sound system, and I used to go at a beach party every Sunday at Gold Coast beach in St Thomas, where I heard him doing 'Wear You To The Ball'. He was talking on the rhythm. While he was talking it sounded like a song to me. So I went to him and I said, 'Could you do that again, that same talking you was doing on the rhythm?' And he did it exactly the same way. Yeah! So I said, 'Wow, this is great! I'm gonna let Duke Reid know about you and know about what you're doing, right, and then I'll contact you and maybe he will make you record it.'

From Osbourne 'King Tubby' Ruddock's studio at 18 Drumilie Avenue in Kingston's rundown Waterhouse neighbourhood emerged music that was artistically revolutionary. Tubby was tragically gunned down on 6th February 1989, the victim of a robbery that went wrong.

"Well, the Monday I told Duke Reid and by Tuesday he sent a brother by the name of Edward to pick up U-Roy and by Tuesday night the song was on tape. That was why he started out with 'Wear You To The Ball', 'cause that was the track that really had me going."

Although U-Roy's earliest deejaying was over tracks by the Paragons, he remembers events slightly differently - yet he agrees that as soon as he encountered Reid, the legendary producer put him into the Treasure Isle studio: "My first recording that I did for him was 'This Station

Below: Dennis Alcapone's pseudonym originated on a trip to the cinema. "When I get the name Alcapone, it all started the night I went to the movies at Majesty Theatre and I was laughing. And the guy say to me, 'Look how him going like a pocony'. Whatever pocony is, I don't know. Then someone change it to Me Capone and then Macaroni. Until someone just start calling me Capone. Then I pick up Alcapone from that. And it just stick."

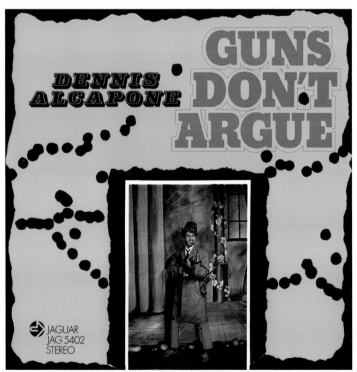

Rule The Nation' and 'Wake The Town And Tell The People'... And then, maybe about another six weeks, 'Wear You To The Ball' was out. Before that came out, 'This Station Rule The Nation' and 'Wake The Town And Tell The People' were number one and two on the radio stations. Then 'Wear You To The Ball' take off 'Wake The Town' and put it at two, and 'Rule the Nation' at three. That was a time when many people started hearing more about me."

The mainstream of the music had very recently shifted to the reggae beat, yet deejays were about to ensure the longevity of rocksteady by recording over its classic rhythms: did the deejays' revived popularity reflect the public's deep-seated fondness for rocksteady?

U-Roy was about to enjoy the benefits from such impeccable taste; for on him had fallen the task of becoming another of Jamaica's truly original innovators: "When I started, nobody know anything about deejay music and things like that. It wasn't much recognised. No Jamaican music was recognised much worldwide at that time, ya know, and I'm really surprised at what I'm seeing now: because there was no sign that this music would be that appreciated by people. It's a very big surprise."

The story of Jamaican deejays is also the story of dub.

The word 'dub' was an abbreviation of 'overdub', the process in which additional instrumental or vocal tracks are added to what already has been recorded. In the same way that the word has been abbreviated from its source, so its meaning in this Jamaican context is reversed. Tracks are subtracted and removed from what has already been recorded: the vocal and parts of a tune's instrumentation are dropped in and out of the mix, at unexpected or seemingly inappropriate moments.

Very early dub, which began at the end of the 1960s, was usually an instrumental which emphasised the drum and bass element by partially removing the organ, piano and guitars.

In the USA or UK the record producer is generally a hands-on, studio knob-twiddler, assisted by an engineer. But in Jamaica the role of the record producer is more that of a film producer, a person who puts creative people and deals together.

Figures like King Tubby, Lee Perry and Errol Thompson, revered as record producers by First World reggae fans, were generally referred to as 'engineers' in Jamaica - as Errol 'T' Thompson always was to producer Joe Gibbs, for example. Even in Jamaica, these terms were not always exclusive; Scratch Perry could be engineer or producer: it was just a question of which hat he would be wearing on any given day.

It was, however, these three engineers in particular - King Tubby, Perry and Thompson - who developed a technique that was to have a lasting effect not only on reggae, but also on all modern dance music. Hot new tunes were cut onto one-off acetate discs (known as 'dubs' or 'dub plates') for use by sound systems, to be played twenty or thirty times before wearing out, in order to popularise a tune in advance of its release.

"But dub music on a whole, was started by King Tubby's," said Dennis Alcapone. "Tubby would buy the acetate from Duke Reid and Coxsone. Buy the raw rhythm on a dub-plate. And when that play in the dancehall it cause a big riot. It was something new. You'd be playing the vocal off a song. And then you lick it again. And it come, and all of a sudden you're hearing no voice. Then the dancehall explode pure noise and thing. Everybody love that. I remember one time I was on the mike, and a man fire off a gunshot behind me, and the mike pick up the shot and just echo it through the dance. And the crowd go crazy.

"When U-Roy come a new sound was born, just like him say, 'Wake The Town And Tell The People'. Because we wake up one morning, and there was U-Roy, mashing up the whole place. And that's how the whole deejay business was really born. U-Roy was with Tubby, but U-Roy was riding the rocksteady rhythms. Like myself, I came up on the rocksteady rhythms. The drum and bass thing, like U-Roy come on. That's when it change over."

Above left: Glen 'God Son' Brown was a supreme example of that Jamaican manner in which those who have nothing are not afraid to be themselves. After having been singer for the Sonny Bradshaw Group, Brown came to personify the island's hand-to-mouth, but deeply innovative, backyard producers during the course of the 1970s: he worked with vocalists including Johnny Clarke and Gregory Isaacs, but more with such deejays as U-Roy, I-Roy, Big Youth and Prince Jazzbo. He would hand his 'versions' over to the 'baldhead-at-the-control' himself, King Tubby, and was the first to credit Osbourne Ruddock on a record, *Tubby's At The Control.*

Right: A friend of Scratch Perry, and similarly driven by economic necessity, Bunny 'Striker' Lee would book the same studio as his spar, and they would run their sessions back-to-back. "Bunny Lee just listens to it and knows," said Aston 'Family Man' Barrett. "In making the updating of Studio One or Treasure Isle tracks a common practice, Bunny Lee anticipated not only the approaches of Channel One and Joe Gibbs, but the dancehall revolution of the next decade," said 'Professor' Steve Barrow.

Lee 'Scratch' Perry, born in Kingston in 1939, graduated from being a 'selecter' on the Downbeat sound system and a 'fetcher' for Coxsone Dodd to a far more formidable figure following a notoriously acrimonious split with Dodd. Bob Marley would drop into Perry's shop, Upsetter Records, on Charles Street to check out this extrovert figure who delighted in word-play. Some people have attributed the birth of reggae to Scratch alone after he started dabbling with a music pace that made you feel, he said, as though you were stepping in glue. He had an international hit in 1969 with 'Return Of Django' by The Upsetters, his house band. The Upsetters, formerly known as The Hippy Boys, had been formed by bass player Aston 'Family Man' Barrett: when Family Man linked up with Lee Perry, the producer decided to make the bass the lead instrument of this new form of reggae in which he was now working.

"Lee Perry had the ears as to what the street people were listening to. Any kinky thing happening, he would immediately know: 'Mr Brown ride through town in a coffin'. He and Bob would get together and laugh about it, and say 'What is this? What is going on there?' And then the two of them get together and b-a-n-g: it's a song, it's a hit, it's what's happening in the street. They had a chemistry."
RITA MARLEY

How did you first meet Coxsone Dodd?

Coxsone was doing dancehall music and I used to be a dancer, as a physical exercise - for energy, for sustaining of the body. So I always train music for exercising. In those days I just wanted to try singing, because I have ideas, and Coxsone was the one who gave me the first try.

So you began making records like 'Roast Duck'?

Rude songs. Scratch songs. 'Roast duck' mean back when yuh fuckin' and all those things. I am extremely slack. Mentally dirty.

And you would go into the studio to work with singers like Delroy Wilson?

I would go with any singer that Selassie-I inspire I to go in the studio with. People regard the flesh as everything, but the flesh is no thing. The flesh made of earth, dust and ashes. But it is the spirit that moves the soul and fire. So when the CIA send an agent to kill His Majesty, the Emperor Selassie in Africa, they did not know that it is not flesh that he is in. I am not mad: I am introducing God.

"This is a dream come true. Come to Jamaica and buy your tourist books and see your dream come true. Come to Kingston, Jamaica, and buy your magic books and love magic. Love studio magic, love radio magic, love camera magic, love television magic, and love revelation of magic magic."

Then you were with West Indies Records - tunes like 'People Funny Boy'.

The idea is about people funny.

One hundred per cent of the human beings on this planet are flesh and blood. They want to use people for their ideas and their thoughts, and their gifts and their talents and their blessings. Which I find extraordinarily, wickedly funny.

And then you started the Upsetter label?

Yes, to upset, to involve

in a musical Armageddon war. The Upsetter label don't come to upset the dance people, because the dance people are here to dance, and to chant down Babylon. The Upsetter label come to upset leaders of government, the council of churches, the politicians and the gunmen and the gunboys, and all evil forces. Upsetter Records come to upset the seven devils and all the demons, all evil and corrupted souls and spirits. The Upsetter not come to fight against flesh and blood.

What inspired you to build your renowned Black Ark studio?

Black heart, black ark.

They are searching for a Noah ark. But there was no Noah ark. That is created by a white man because they want to fool somebody. N-O is no and A-H mean pain. So it mean no pain.

You made some great work there.

It wasn't my work.
I just playing the part.

I am an instrument of the Master, Computer XIX. It wasn't I who make the sound - I was just being the engineer. I am the music dolly: it is the music who do it. The music is my daddy. Just as Jah live and Jah wise. Okay?

I can't take the praises:

the praises go elsewhere, to the most high God. Croaking Lizard. And the Blackboard Jungle. Now we in the jungle, but no one play the part of Peter Pan. Return to the jungle: I put it in my thought that I can fly, and I can fly. Musically [laughs].

MAD PROFESSOR

You made the Blackboard Jungle *LP with King Tubby. How did you come to meet him?*

He come to me because Tubby looking for adventure,

and I am the only adventurer. And Tubby was looking for that adventure that turn him from a sperm to a baby, and he see the adventure and know that it is a lively adventure and that it is God's adventure. Dub adventure. I thought he was my student, and he thought I was his student. But it makes no matter. It makes no difference - I'm not jealous. The facts you are looking for is all under my jungle boots.

The studio was a four-track studio?

It was only four of it on the machine,

but I was picking up twenty. From the extra-terrestrial squad. That make me mad. I was so glad to meet that extra-terrestrial squad. Then I draw my rod and interpret it and inter-mediate the politicians that impersonate God. Egypt is a lesson. It is a memory, a total mega-memory, of an experience I had, way back in the jungle, as a baby. It is with me in the spirit, brother, believe you me.

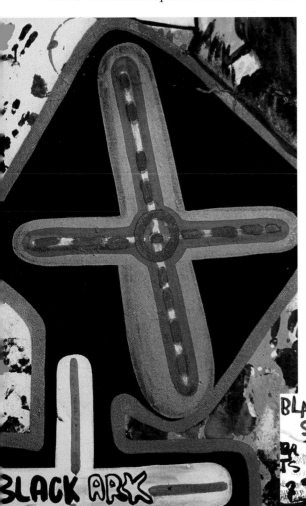

How would you work in those days?

Any power is given to me by the music.

If I want to obeah one, I just obeah them musically; if I want to voodoo them, I voodoo them musically; if I want to execute anybody, I execute them musically; if I want to exterminate anybody, I exterminate them musically; if I want to liquidate anybody, I liquidate them. Everyone has their own world, and I have my world: my world is not visible, it is invisible.

In the early days of the Upsetters, you were working with musicians like Glen Adams who used to be a singer and then turned to the organ.

I don't know much about his early days.

But I was looking for some new musicians. I am so easy to bore it is a shame: there is no pleasure in boredness, you understand? So I name my own game, and the young kids are looking for their own games. That is how they are coming to me.

How would you describe dub music?

As the master of the universe,

the master of the elements, the master of the comets, the master of magic, the master of logic, the master of science, the master of the earth, the master of the air, the master of the water, the master of fire. Hare Krishna Hari Rama, Shiva Sai Baba, Emperor Ras Tafari, the truth cutter.

Music make the dubs.

I am the dub shepherd. I can't give myself no praises, I give praise to the God who create the God of Gods. I give praise to the one who is over all.

What was it like working with Bob Marley?

It was very fuckin' great fun.

But I had a sixth sense from a vision coming up. It said, 'Don't let a politician do you a favour: they will always want to control you forever'. And that was his biggest mistake: he wasn't listening to what I was writing. He was good to work with - number one. I couldn't find a better agent than that. Better agents than that don't come from the earth. ## My love.

Around 1968 Dennis Alcapone had started his own small sound, El Paso, named after the ballad by Marty Robbins, the American country-and-western singer, a great influence on many Jamaican vocalists (the melodic songs of modern 'conscious' star Luciano are clearly inspired by Robbins, as the singer admits). El Paso was based in the rough Kingston neighbourhood of Waltham Park Road. For Dennis Smith, as he then was, there was only one sound, the one with which U-Roy would take the mike, the one that mashed up the whole of the island: King Tubby's Hometown Hi-Fi. "Tubby's was definitely the greatest sound ever to come out of Jamaica, in terms of the arrangements and the equipment and everything else," the deejay told writer David Katz for *People Funny Boy*, the authorised biography of Lee 'Scratch' Perry. "The technology and everything was just mind-boggling really. Them time, when you listen to King Tubby's sound, it looks like it going to blow your mind."

One of Tubby's many secret weapons was his mission to bring a different bass sound to the dance. "His bass was something else, it was just round like when you are kneading flour: Tubby's, the bass was just solid. Then he brought in reverb, which wasn't introduced to the public before, reverb and echo."

By 1970 Dennis Alcapone was himself recording, as exemplified on his *Forever Version* LP, recorded for Coxsone Dodd, in which he makes the fullest use of Studio One rhythms: the fantastic deejay title track, for example, is a version of Carlton and his Shoes' equally great 'Love Me Forever', whilst Delroy Wilson's 'Run Run', the Heptones' 'Hypnotic Baby' and Alton Ellis's superb 'Sunday Coming' are among the other tunes over which Dennis chats. Soon he was the number two deejay in Jamaica, after U-Roy.

The dub phenomenon did not really get into its stride until 1972, by which time King Tubby had upgraded his dub-cutting studio to four-track and was mixing tunes for such producers as Bunny Lee, Glen Brown and Lee Perry. Using the mixing console as a form of musical instrument, Tubby and engineers from other studios (among them Errol Thompson, Sylvan Morris and Sid Bucknor) started to experiment and re-arrange rhythms by dropping instruments in and out of the now drum and bass-dominated mix. Splashes of reverb and layers of repeat echo, which became a signifying sound of dub, would be added to great effect.

Dub continued to grow in popularity to the point where the dub mixes were credited as A-sides, and whole albums of dub tracks, once only pressed in limited quantities for sound system use, became best sellers. There is much argument as to which was the first dub LP specifically created as such. *Upsetters 14 Dub Blackboard Jungle* - more widely known as *Blackboard Jungle Dub* - is often claimed as the first

Near right: With his master engineer Errol 'T' Thompson, Joe 'Gibbs' Gordon could create both the quality pop of 'Uptown Top Ranking' (he used the same rhythm for Trinity's equally fabulous 'Three Piece Suit', a sort of deejay answer record), or the masterful and rootsy *Africa Dub* series. Gibbs was one of the prime motivators of the Disco-45 phenomenon, twelve-inch singles featuring several 'versions'.
Right: Augustus Pablo at the Channel One studios.

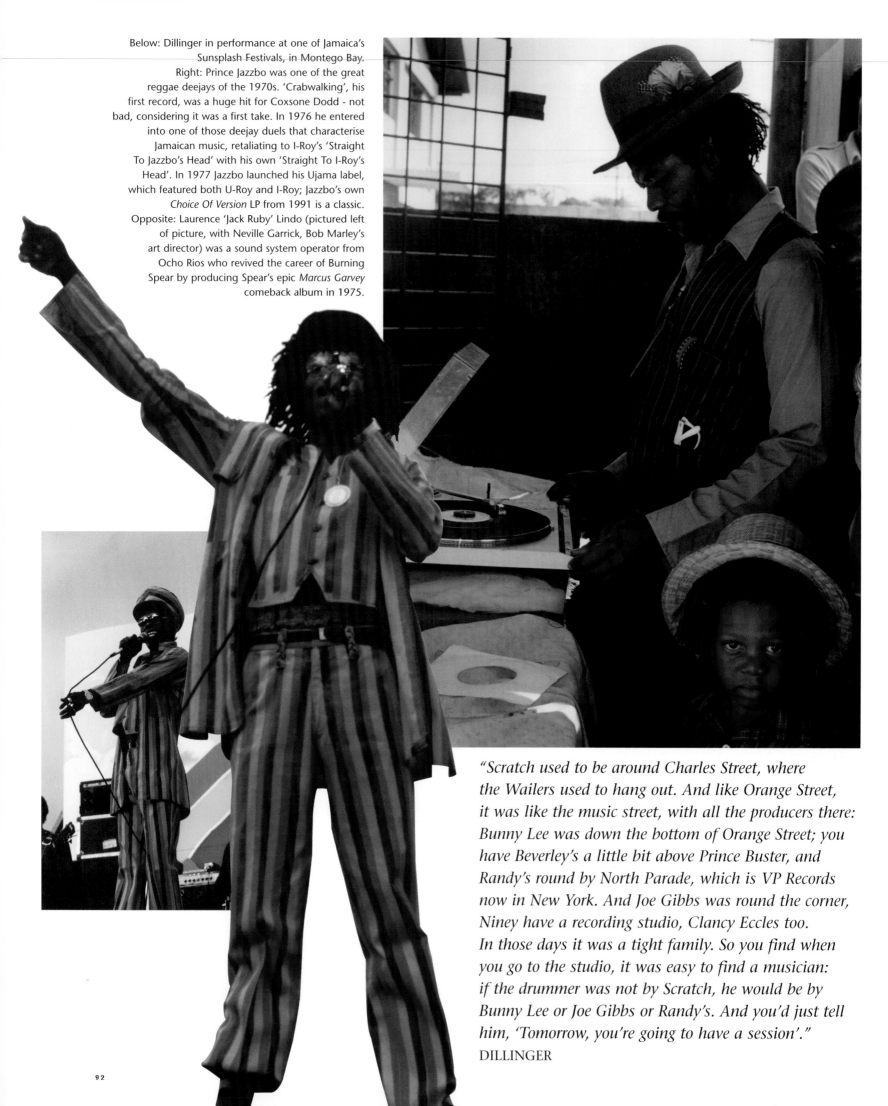

Below: Dillinger in performance at one of Jamaica's Sunsplash Festivals, in Montego Bay.
Right: Prince Jazzbo was one of the great reggae deejays of the 1970s. 'Crabwalking', his first record, was a huge hit for Coxsone Dodd - not bad, considering it was a first take. In 1976 he entered into one of those deejay duels that characterise Jamaican music, retaliating to I-Roy's 'Straight To Jazzbo's Head' with his own 'Straight To I-Roy's Head'. In 1977 Jazzbo launched his Ujama label, which featured both U-Roy and I-Roy; Jazzbo's own *Choice Of Version* LP from 1991 is a classic.
Opposite: Laurence 'Jack Ruby' Lindo (pictured left of picture, with Neville Garrick, Bob Marley's art director) was a sound system operator from Ocho Rios who revived the career of Burning Spear by producing Spear's epic *Marcus Garvey* comeback album in 1975.

"Scratch used to be around Charles Street, where the Wailers used to hang out. And like Orange Street, it was like the music street, with all the producers there: Bunny Lee was down the bottom of Orange Street; you have Beverley's a little bit above Prince Buster, and Randy's round by North Parade, which is VP Records now in New York. And Joe Gibbs was round the corner, Niney have a recording studio, Clancy Eccles too. In those days it was a tight family. So you find when you go to the studio, it was easy to find a musician: if the drummer was not by Scratch, he would be by Bunny Lee or Joe Gibbs or Randy's. And you'd just tell him, 'Tomorrow, you're going to have a session'."
DILLINGER

dub album, although Prince Buster's *The Message* and Clive Chinn's *Java Java* emerged at around the same time. The Scratch record was a compilation of fourteen of the hardest recent Upsetter dubs: 'Black Panta' was a dub of 'Bucky Skank'; 'African Skank' was a version of Junior Byles' 'Place Called Africa'; and 'Moving Skank' a version of 'Keep On Moving' by the Wailers, who had recorded the original as part of the sessions with Perry. The same group's 'Dreamland' became 'Dreamland Skank' and 'Kaya' became 'Kaya Skank'.

Whether or not *Blackboard Jungle Dub* was the true originator, it certainly helped inaugurate the genre of dub albums. During the latter half of the 1970s many producers and studios furthered their reputations by making classic dub reggae, including Channel One, Joe Gibbs, Lee Perry, Bunny Lee and Augustus Pablo. Through records like the classic *King Tubby Meets Rockers Uptown*, artists like Augustus Pablo, the brilliant melodica-player,

became irrevocably associated with a style whose merits were enhanced when the disc was played at spine-thudding volume at a sound system dance.

Dub albums poured out of Kingston in the second half of the 1970s. It also became the protocol for acts to release dub equivalents of their official LPs - *Garvey's Ghost*, the Jack Ruby-engineered dub of Burning Spear's already ground-breaking *Marcus Garvey* was a classic of the genre when it was released in 1976. Meanwhile, Joe Gibbs famously entered the fray with his celebrated Errol T-engineered *Africa Dub* series.

If sound system music had always been considered low-rent, deejay music was seen as virtually the shanty-town of Jamaican music - appropriately, as it gave hope to many a ghetto youth with no formal musical training. It was not Dennis Alcapone alone who caught U-Roy's slipstream. Increasingly, through the 1970s, Jamaican records featured men-on-the-mike and the decade echoed to their sound.

Above: At first the reputation of Tapper Zukie, the man from Rema, was far greater in the UK and USA than in Jamaica. He cut his 1973 reputation-forging first LP, *Man A Warrior*, in England, where the Ethnic/Fight label owner Larry Lawrence, knowing of the toaster's reputation from his deejay residency with the Virgo sound system, recorded him for the first time. Zukie's 'MPLA' 45 was the largest-selling UK deejay hit of 1976, taken up by the likes of punk star Patti Smith.
Opposite: Photographer Adrian Boot first met Mikey Dread when Dread was a pupil at Titchfield School in Port Antonio, where Boot was himself teaching. The next time they met was with the Clash at a record company party in London's Camden - Dread was taken up by the group and toured with them, toasting on a couple of numbers. A former radio DJ in Jamaica, who became a recording deejay, he later worked for Radio Bristol in the UK.

Names like Prince Jazzbo, Tapper Zukie, Prince Far-I, the self-producing Dr Alimantado, Ranking Joe and Mikey Dread became staples of Jamaican music.

In the mid-1970s close friends Wade Brammer, aka Trinity, and Lester Bullocks, aka Dillinger, developed a more commercial, smoother style and led reggae into the age of the 12-inch disco-mix, the 'Disco 45': originally an American innovation, the idea was to cut a louder and longer record than on a 7-inch single. Jamaican producers soon realised that the format was eminently suited to the established reggae custom of playing a vocal song, which would be followed by the deejay version, often with a dub mix to follow.

The 12-inch disco could hold at least the vocal and deejay cuts on one side, although attempts to splice the two together were frequently hamfisted.

One tune of the mid-1970s that has become almost a standard is 'Cocaine In My Brain' by Dillinger: the song's subject matter made it a staple of New York clubs like Studio 54, and to this day it is part of the soundtrack, in various re-mixed forms, of many a nightclub around the world. Its success prompted Dillinger to record a follow-up song entitled 'Marijuana In My Brain' - unsurprisingly, this became a number one hit in liberal-minded Holland.

'Cocaine In My Brain' was a track from *CB 200*, Dillinger's second album, which he had recorded at Channel One for Jo Jo Hookim, the studio's owner. As well as the 'Cocaine' song and the almost equally celebrated title track - a reference to a model of Honda motorcycle that was considered to be highly desirable in mid-1970s Jamaica - that LP contained several other hits, including 'Crank Face' and 'Plantation Heights'.

There was a specific triumvirate of deejays whose **chatting over records paved the way for the development of rap music in the United States.** Alongside **U-Roy** (right) the threesome was completed by his **near-namesake I-Roy** (left) and **Big Youth.**

From the Waltham Park Road area of Kingston, Lester 'Dillinger' Bullocks had been given his *nom de disque* by Lee 'Scratch' Perry. "At first I was trying to sound like Dennis Alcapone," said Dillinger. "When I was going to the studio, I was saying, 'My name is Alcapone Junior, but Scratch Perry take me to the studio at Dynamic, and when I come to do my track, he say, 'What is your name?' I say, 'I am Alcapone Junior'. He say, 'No, you are not, you are Dillinger'. Scratch give me that name."

At first, Dillinger had wanted to be a singer. But when he went to one of Coxsone Dodd's regular Sunday auditions he was told to come back in two years' time. "I couldn't wait. I was in a rush, so I said I will be a deejay now. You have only a few deejays in those days, so it was quicker to cross over in the deejay section.

"And I was inspired by Dennis Alcapone and U-Roy: El Paso sound, King Tubby's Hi-Fi, King Edward's, Duke Reid the Trojan, and Sir Coxsone Downbeat. One of my relatives was a dancehall promoter. So as lickle kids we were there to pick up the bottle and put it in the crates. And eventually we would get to listen to the music and to the sound system."

For Coxsone Dodd, Dillinger recorded *Ready Natty Dreadie,* an extraordinary first album. "Before the Channel One era. The Coxsone one is like it's for all time. It still sound good. I used lots of old rhythms, like Alton Ellis, like the Real Rock rhythm. When I go in the studio and they put on the rhythm, I request sometimes a song I really like, like a Delroy Wilson. And them say, 'That one sound like you can do it'. But usually producer call you and say they want you to toast over this rhythm."

I-Roy first developed his rich vocal style - sly, funny, and often pruriently knowing - when working with several of the island's sound systems. Roy Samuel Reid, as he was christened, was first employed as an accountant in the Jamaican Department of Customs and Excise. A music fan with an income sufficient to let him indulge his tastes, he began to work with the Soul Bunnies disco in Kingston in 1966. "Dat man 'ave logic," he claimed the audience would cheer the frequently hilarious introductions and comments with which he would spice up instrumental tunes; a lover of story-telling, and all the embellishments he could bring to it, Reid found himself in his natural role as a technological *griot.*

By 1969 Roy Reid had re-named himself I-Roy, partially as a witty rejoinder to U-Roy. He began working on the Son's Junior sound system in Spanish Town, soon moving to Ruddy's S-R-S, the number one Spanish Town 'sound': over tunes from artists like Alton Ellis and the Heptones, I-Roy would extemporise scat chants; for example:
"My cash disbursement is without contentment/So come on down yah/For the heatment is greatment/In this compartment."

After hearing 'Wake The Town', U-Roy's innovative first record, 'toasting' on a classic Treasure Isle rock steady tune, I-Roy recorded 'Musical Pleasure' and 'Drifter' both of which sold strongly for producer Harry Mudie. He followed them with a version of the Ebony Sisters' 'Let Me Tell You Boy' and Dennis Walks' 'Margaret', becoming a

Below: Clint Eastwood, the brother of fellow deejay Trinity, was to enjoy stardom in the UK when Junjo Lawes paired him with General Saint for their version of Queen's 'Another One Bites The Dust', which launched a successful career on the UK and European college circuit.

Opposite: Jah Stitch began his career on Tippertone Hi-Fi, the same sound that featured Big Youth. In 1976 he left to start a set of his own, Black Harmony, and Stitch jokingly announced he would destroy Tippertone. A pair of Tippertone supporters chased Stitch through Bob Marley's Tuff Gong Record Shop on King Street and into the yard next door where they shot him in the head. Somehow the deejay survived and was soon in Tubby's studio, recording 'No Dread Can Dead' for Bunny Lee. Stitch's *Original Ragga Muffin (1975-77)* set on Blood and Fire is masterly.

familiar figure in Kingston as he distributed his discs on a Honda S-90 motorcycle. Celebrated as the most intelligent of all deejays, I-Roy would drop references to such cultural icons as Mickey Spillane, Alfred Hitchcock and Cleopatra.

I-Roy began to deejay for King Tubby's Home Town Hi-Fi - although I-Roy quit in 1973 after defending a girl from a man who was trying to rape her behind a speaker box. By now he had recorded for most of the name producers in Jamaica, including Lee Perry, Winston 'Merritone' Blake, Lloyd Charmers, Keith Hudson, and Bunny Lee; and for Gussie Clarke he recorded his first album, the superb *Presenting I-Roy*. His tunes were never far from the top of the charts in Jamaica, also selling strongly amongst the ethnic communities of England and the USA. After the split with King Tubby, he came to London in 1974 and took up a residency at the celebrated Roaring Twenties club in Carnaby Street.

Returning to Jamaica in 1975 I-Roy then struck up an alliance with Jojo Hookim's Channel One studio; his 'Welding' tune proved a big hit and he subsequently became the studio's house producer, working on such legendary numbers as 'MPLA'. That same year, the ever entertaining I-Roy entered into a musical feud with Prince Jazzbo of the kind that peppers the history of Jamaican music: and I-Roy's 'Straight To Jazzbo's Head' was answered with Jazzbo's 'Straight To I-Roy's Head'.

In 1976, I-Roy signed an album deal with Virgin Records, and recorded five albums for the label, including 1977's splendid *Heart Of A Lion*. "I used to really enjoy it when I-Roy would come round and hold court," said Jumbo Van Renen, his A&R man at the label. "He was so funny and quite evidently a thinker. I would tell him you could make half a dozen records from each of those visits."

Following close behind U-Roy and I-Roy were the chatting talents of Manley Augustus Buchanan, better known as Big Youth. Big Youth represented an even rootsier approach, combining everyday street talk with religious and political lyrics, often adapted from Last Poets records who he cited as an influence equivalent to John Coltrane and the Beatles.

Big Youth set the style for the next decade of deejays, both as an originator of what became known as rap and later of 'singjay', where he would literally sing his chants.

How did you get started?

It was a time when there was nothing much that people were saying. A conflicting and confusing time.

We need more inspiration, more than "*baby, baby*". That was when Big Youth come in with the whole Jah Love thing. I come with a Rasta kind of set, a poetical, spiritual form where you tell people let's make love and not war, and come together.

The resident deejay with the Lord Tippertone sound system in the early 1970s, Big Youth rose quickly to become one of the most iconic 'chatters' of all time. Produced by Keith Hudson in 1972, Big Youth's 'S.90 Skank' was a number one Jamaican hit for weeks: "*Don't you ride like lightning/Or you'll crash like thunder,*" he declared. With his front teeth inlaid with red, gold and green gems, Big Youth rivalled Bob Marley in Jamaica for popularity. *Screaming Target* was an epochal album, featuring rhythms by Gregory Isaacs and Dennis Brown. Forming his own Negusa Nagast and Augustus Buchanan labels, he put out a flood of fantastic records. Hugely influential on modern-day reggae and rap, Big Youth is one of the great innovators.

Tippertone was the first set you came to prominence with.

Yes, Tippertone is an old town sound

- downtown Kingston in Princes Street, Matthews Lane and all those places. One night we went to a dance in Papine. We see a sound with I-Roy the President playing, and someone steal all the records and the deejay was afraid to turn up. He took the mike with the Satta Massa Gana and created a whole scene.

That's when we knew something was developing. Hear this: it not like a boast -

I never exalt upon my name, but if someone come and try and play against me on Tippertone, it's like you're coming to challenge Mohammed Ali and you can't beat the man. Then with Gregory Isaacs I went to the studio and did 'Movie Star' and 'Black Cinderella'. And Gussie came by and we do 'The Killer' for Joe Gibbs. Another Friday Keith Hudson came and we did a record that went straight to number one: 'S-90 Skank'.

By the mid-70s you had your own production thing going.

Yes. Because at one time I had seven songs in both charts, with five in the two Top Tens - 1 and

2, 4, 5, 6. They call me phenomenon. But with all this there was nothing much happening for me financially. So I did a cover version of 'War', and called it 'Streets In Africa'. Which was a different thing from toasting: it was singing this time. There was a lot of people who say, "Oh boy, you can't sing", but financially I was better with that song than being what they said I could do for other people. That was when I started develop with the 'African Daughter', 'Hit The Road Jack', 'Every Nigger Is A Star'.

These records established you as a different kind of deejay from the likes of U-Roy.

Definitely. It's a revolution of naturality. It's not something like you put on. One

great thing is not to lose common touch with the people. I live with the people. I seen violence and strife in the city, and mischief in the streets. I see people that they say is bad who I know is good people.

Inspiration go through the vibrations of the time. Statements

come when you get rhythm. Even today I have song after song written inside of me.

I believe in the Almighty.

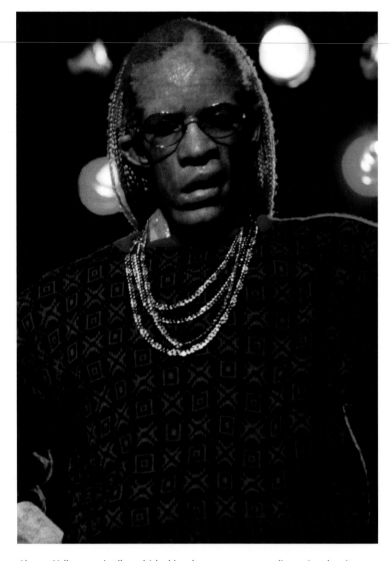

Above: Yellowman's alleged 'slack' style was not as one-dimensional as it appeared. In that way typical of Jamaican art, there was always a spiritual underplay, as his general 'rudeness' also contained much irony. Coming immediately after the death of Bob Marley, Yellowman's success appeared to mark a downward slide for Jamaican music, but time shows it was more complex than that.

Opposite: In 1992 and 1993 Chaka Demus and Pliers were themselves briefly the biggest Jamaican recording artists in the world: with rhythms courtesy of Sly and Robbie, the combination of vocalist Pliers (right in picture) and deejay Chaka Demus enjoyed six UK hits off their *Tease Me* album, including the fabulously addictive title track and 'Murder She Wrote'.

Big Youth's first album was for Prince Buster - or, rather, it was one-third of an album, *Chi Chi Run*, filled out with tunes from Dennis Brown, John Holt and Alton Ellis, and instrumentals from Buster's All Stars.

Keith Hudson had already produced U-Roy, Dennis Alcapone, and I-Roy. Then he turned his hand to the new toasting sensation Big Youth, giving him his first major hit with 'S.90 Skank', a tribute to the Honda motorcycle, which was hugely popular in Jamaica - Hudson installed a bike in the studio, and revved it up to give the requisite atmosphere. For 'S.90 Skank' Big Youth toasted over the rhythm of 'True True To My Heart', a track which Hudson himself had sung on.

Screaming Target, however, was the first great LP released by Big Youth. Produced by Gussie Clarke (at around 20 years old, of a similar age to Youth), the rhythms that the record used included those for Leroy Smart's 'Pride And Ambition', Gregory Isaacs' 'One One Cocoa Fill Basket', K.C. White's 'No, No, No' and Lloyd Parks' 'Slaving'. "Clint Eastwood had the film with *Dirty Harry*, which was a crazy gun movie," recalled Big Youth. "Then someone came up with a film called *Screaming Target* and this gunman was even crazier than Clint Eastwood deal with. I just make fun of it, that *Screaming Target* was renker than *Dirty Harry*. Because if you check the song 'Screaming Target', it is a song which is teaching people not to be illiterate, 'cause they must go to a literate place and get civilised. So it is really a education of a song." Big Youth's chanting style set the standard for the following decade of deejays; he also personified the 'roots' style that came to be a central theme of reggae from the mid-1970s.

As the 1980s developed, deejaying became recognised as being as important as any other feature of reggae music. New styles were developed and mastered. For example, Anthony 'Lone Ranger' Waldron, who had spent much of his youth in the UK, was an inspiration from when he first started recording in the late 1970s, working first with Studio One and then Alvin Ranglin: he enjoyed major success in 1980 with 'Barnabas Collins', a vampire song that included the line "*Chew ya neck like a Wrigley's*". It was the Lone Ranger who introduced the addictive vocal interjections - "*ribbit!*", "*oink!* and "*bim!*" - that became a staple of deejay music in the first half of the 1980s.

The cultural themes of artists like Big Youth, meanwhile, were coming up against a sweeping mood of sexual lubricity, a contradiction that always would run hand-in-hand in 'dancehall', a style that first developed in 1979. That year, for example, General Echo released an album produced by Winston Riley entitled *The Slackest*, that ironically led to Echo's delivery being compared in originality and influence to that of Big Youth. The record was followed by Echo's *12 Inches Of Pleasure* album, whose subject-matter is even more self-explanatory, and which was produced by Junjo Lawes, the father of dancehall. As though to prove that such subject-matter was part of the *zeitgeist*, 1980 saw the release of the *Sex Education* album by Trinity's brother Clint Eastwood, who had previously recorded such reality LPs as *African Youth*.

Even though there had been portents, it was still a shock - and one from which many fans of reggae in the 1970s have never recovered - when, following the death of Bob Marley on 11th May 1981, Jamaican music became newly personified by the figure of Yellowman.

Like the mixed-race Bob, Winston 'Yellowman' Foster was also an outsider - outcast, more like, which is the fate in Jamaica of many of those born with the albino skin that earned Yellowman his name. From this distance it is hard to recall the extent of Yellowman's popularity in the first years of the 1980s. But for a short while he was unquestionably the best-known living Jamaican recording artist, partially because of the way in which 'King Yellow' deliberately made play of what he didn't have going for him: in 1982 Yellowman released 16 albums, the songs on most of which concerned his limitless sex appeal and prowess, a dark irony appreciated by his audience, and enhanced by the monotone of his delivery. His popularity was assisted by the production of several of his records being overseen by Junjo Lawes, who had an unerring ear for the appropriate dancehall sound.

By 1984 Yellowman was on the wane, a victim perhaps of his own over-production. Appearing immediately in the wake of Bob Marley, however, Yellowman set the tone for the future of Jamaican music. During the course of the 1980s, the style of Jamaican deejays and US rap artists gradually grew closer together. By the time the music went digital, around the time that 'Yellow' fell from grace, apparently arrogant deejays - whose ironic complexities were often missed - had become the norm: the boasting and *braggadocio* of Shabba Ranks, which formed part of the armoury with which he attained success in the late 1980s and early 1990s, was only a development of the mood of the decade.

As the millennium turned deejays were still going strong, with artists like Beenie Man, Bounty Killer, Buju Banton, Capleton and Mr Vegas representing different facets of the genre - and some of the early deejay pioneers being given fresh opportunities to record and tour.

The most important development had been the enormous influence that deejay reggae had had on Black American youth, who effectively took back the style, combined it with elements nearer to home and proceeded to invent it as 'rap' - the biggest selling black music in the world today.

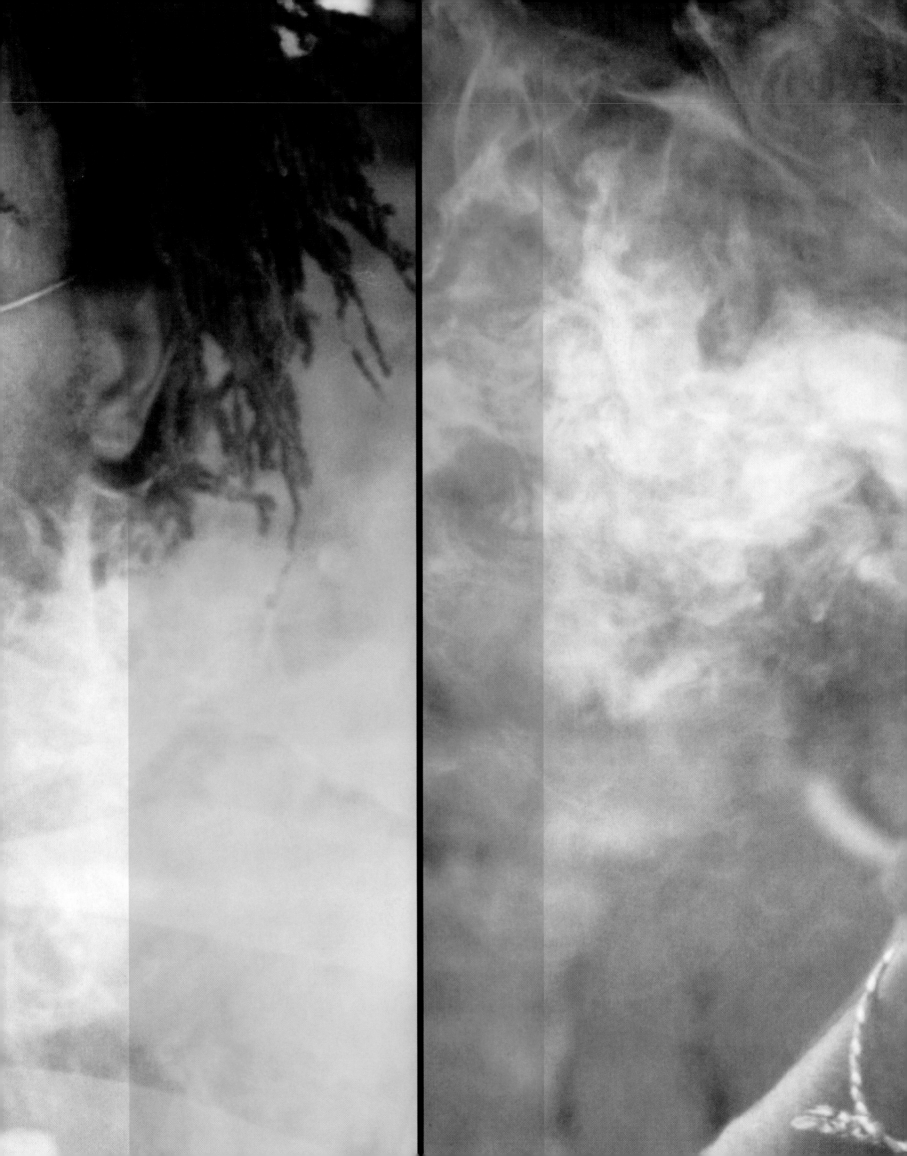

For international public consumption, Bob Marley was the personification of roots rock reggae and of the interlinked Rastafari, the bringer of news to the world of **Jah, Haile Selassie,** and the power of the **red, gold and green** Ethiopian flag. But it was not just Bob alone: at Lee 'Scratch' Perry's Black Ark studio, for example, reasonings about the Bible would

ROOTS ROCK

take place every day. In the mid-1970s, listening to reggae was like being initiated into an **arcane area of history.** The potent, fiery iconography of Rastafari - overstood by the archetypal image of H.I.M. Haile Selassie I - was omnipresent in those days, even crossing over into the realms of punk rock, with which reggae in the UK joined forces as **a soundtrack of the dispossessed.**

As Kingston became increasingly ungovernable during this period, the countryside inland seemed a more agreeable place for a man wishing to partake of **a little herb to aid his meditations**. Rasta elders congregated in settlements deep in the bush, from which the sound of 'nyabinghi' drumming would resonate.

REGGAE

When Burning Spear called his second Island LP *Man Of The Hills,* it was as if he was setting himself up as the quintessence of Roots Rasta culture. For **the soul of Jamaica lies in the Blue Mountains** which dominate the interior of the island: they are like the repository of the nation's collective unconsciousness. The poetry of this movement had a profound and significant power. No wonder Babylon quaked in its boots.

"Scratch, you were into Rastafari, then you became the only person in the world to espouse the religion of Pipecock Jackson, a religion that you invented yourself. But are you still into Rastafari?"

"Art! For it has come to this now: Art!" Scratch pauses for a moment, framed in the bay window of the council house in Edgware, north London in which he is inexplicably living in the autumn of 1987. "How great thou art!"

For most westerners the initial interviews by Bob Marley to promote the *Catch A Fire* album marked the first time they had heard of the apparently curious religion of Rastafarianism. Although this had been common subject-matter in Jamaica for the past forty years, in the 1970s Rastafari took off like a bushfire, partly inspired by the political situation on the island. Its unification of arcane mysticism and radical protest touched a collective nerve in both musicians and audience: and a thought-provoking, underground soundtrack for the decade emerged.

Across the Caribbean, the 1970s was an era of radical change. In Nicaragua, El Salvador, Guatemala and Colombia, left-wing guerrilla groups grew in force, ready for the intensified struggle that would come as the decade turned. The mood also found a resonance in Jamaica. Prime Minister Michael Manley, who came to power in 1972, followed a socialist course that almost guaranteed conflict with the United States - especially when he linked his country's destiny with Cuba, declaring that Third World countries should ally together.

In order to mobilise his forces, Manley had invoked the spirit of the Jamaican black civil rights leader Marcus Garvey, who had founded the Universal Negro Improvement Association in 1914. With prophet-like portentousness, Manley would stride forth amongst his rank-and-file support wielding his 'Rod of Correction', a staff inherited from Garvey. Clearly Michael Manley was in touch with the *zeitgeist*.

Participants in the dreadlocked life of Rastafari in Port Antonio in 1974 (above); an everyday recreational activity in Burning Spear's yard in St Ann's Bay in the mid-1970s (right).

From 1974 onwards, Jamaica was locked in a state of near-civil war, wracked with feuding between the gunmen of the right-wing JLP and its rivals, the incumbent left-wing PNP. The music of the decade mirrored this strife. Much of it was created in what became known as a 'cultural', or 'reality', frame of mind: in other words, the writers and musicians were alert to the social injustices being wrought upon their nation and fellow 'sufferahs'.

The expression of this struggle often bore the full panoply of Rastafarian imagery, although it was sometimes only a cosmetic connection. But the sufferahs, the battle against oppression and the religion of Rastafari became intertwined with the common foe of 'Babylon', essentially the collective evils of the political and economic system.

And in the 1970s images of the inspirationally melancholic Haile Selassie and the red, gold and green of the Ethiopian flag became part of the fabric of reggae. Hardly any LP seemed to be released whose sleeve did not consist of red, gold and green-bordered artwork of the artist in question smoking an enormous sno-cone spliff. Ganja, or 'herb', as it became known, was given divine sanction by Rastafarians because of a somewhat enthusiastic interpretation of certain selected lines in the Bible. It also bestowed upon reggae the appropriate spirit of rebellion necessary for the nurturing of any underground musical movement.

In the mid to late 1970s almost all Jamaican musical artists had grown dreadlocks and were singing about similar culturally-related subject-matter. Only the grimmest, most disadvantaged backgrounds were considered acceptable to snobbish middle-class writers working on British and American music papers: acts like Third World and Inner Circle, with their singer Jacob Miller, incurred disfavour for their moderately privileged backgrounds.

And even the great I-Roy, who favoured big hats and shots of rum as he eyed up the talent lounging by the Sheraton poolside bar, was considered a lesser being in

Emperor Haile Selassie I

Rastafarianism - which has been practised in Jamaica since around 1930 - is essentially a belief in the oldest known form of Christianity, the Ethiopian Orthodox Church, which was allegedly founded when Christ's persecuted disciples fled into the upper Nile area. What can seem baffling about Rastafari are the unformulated, anarchic aspects of the religion - although the distaste for rules in Jamaica should make this thoroughly logical: the individual may apply his personal interpretations and add-ons, of which an inclination to consume large amounts of 'herb' is certainly the best known. Most confusion seems to centre on the worship of Haile Selassie I, the last Emperor of Ethiopia; yet even here nothing is specific. Was Haile Selassie, who is descended from Solomon and Sheba, a first-class prophet? Was he the re-incarnation of Christ? Or was he God himself? Westerners assert that Haile Selassie was a usurious despot, but from the eye-level of Africa and Jamaica he is seen as the one black king who defeated European colonialists.

comparison to the chalice-smoking, dreadlocked U-Roy, notwithstanding the stream of social protest songs I-Roy already had released. Fine 'baldhead' artists like George Faith could hardly get a look in overseas with his superb album *To Be A Lover*, produced by Lee 'Scratch' Perry.

Roots fever gripped the island, where roots music, with its emphasis on spirituality and the inner being, provided some level of counterpoint to the languid everyday acceptance of death and devastation meted out by political gunmen. By the end of 1976, Bob Marley himself had been gunned down in an assassination attempt at his headquarters at 56 Hope Road in uptown Kingston. It seemed impossible to step down a street in the Jamaican capital without your ear being bent by some proselytising Rasta dog soldier. Did these fundamentalists not realise that you had heard exactly the same rap from the last dread with whom you had spoken?

With his landmark *Marcus Garvey* album, produced by Jack Ruby, Burning Spear helped set the agenda in 1975, as well as championing one of Jamaica's national heroes: "*No one remember old Marcus Garvey,*" lamented the first line of the title song. A wonderful, poetic work of mature vision, the album's success built on the reputation that Spear had set in motion with his first Studio One single, 'Door Peep', in 1969, and marked the beginning of a career trajectory that would see Burning Spear indubitably installed as the elder statesman of reggae by the dawning of the 1990s.

The reported death of His Imperial Majesty Haile Selassie I on 27th August 1975 only served to galvanise commitment to Rastafari. The apocalyptic force of this news was felt across the island, increasing the confusion between the metaphorical and the literal: for example, Junior Byles, Scratch Perry's talented protégé, attempted suicide, and was hospitalised in Bellevue. Bob Marley responded in song to this disturbing news straightaway with the stunning 'Jah Live', produced by Lee Perry at Harry J's studio.

To the world outside Jamaica, Bob Marley would come to be seen as the embodiment of the movement, but on the island he was of course but one of many followers of Rastafari. From his Black Ark studio in the Kingston suburb of Washington Gardens, the eccentric Scratch Perry was turning out an endless procession of roots classics; at Black Ark, convoluted 'reasonings' about the Bible would take place every day and sometimes all day. After he had spent two weeks recording there in 1976, the white soul singer Robert Palmer commented that Scratch's studio seemed to be "the spiritual and political centre of the island".

"The whole Rasta concept was to bring unification to mankind through music, y'know. It not a race. Music is a music to bring people together. So all a dat goodness that we was trying to do, preaching love and unity and togetherness... In the 80s they did a review on reggae music, and said that it come to upset western culture, y'unnerstan? And they targeted Marley, and we sight the Gong go down. I watch it. People start to get nasty. In that day you find a lickle youth and say, 'Mek him dread up him dead and show naturality.' But today them lickle baby man they sing them most nasty song and them speak about the most crucialist gun. So that is the love we was bringing, people try to break. All over the years, the seed that I've planted, I still live by it. I still perform my music and try to channel it to the corners in whatever little way. So you know that righteousness uplift a nation and sin is a reproach to man." BIG YOUTH

"Most of my friends throughout my life is Rastafarian. But somehow it didn't attract me. For me to worship a next flesh body as God couldn't pass my head - to me God have to be greater than flesh. And at the same time I was getting some information as to Ethiopia and the doings of Haile Selassie which was in contrast to what I was learning from the Rastas in Jamaica. So I couldn't accept all that. Since all my friends was that I didn't war with them, but they know me - I'm me own man, me don't follow." PRINCE BUSTER

The roots of Burning Spear's early style lay in the **pure music** that would be played at Rastafarian 'grounations', or meetings. This form was known as 'nyabinghi' music, and was based around chanting and drumming on African-type instruments by **the faith's mystical elders.** This was the style of music that Don Drummond would disappear into the Wareika hills to listen to, when it was performed by such adepts as Ras Michael and the Sons of Negus or Count Ossie and the Mystic Revelation of Rastafari, whose *Grounation* triple album was the first example of this **deep roots style** heard by many reggae novitiates.

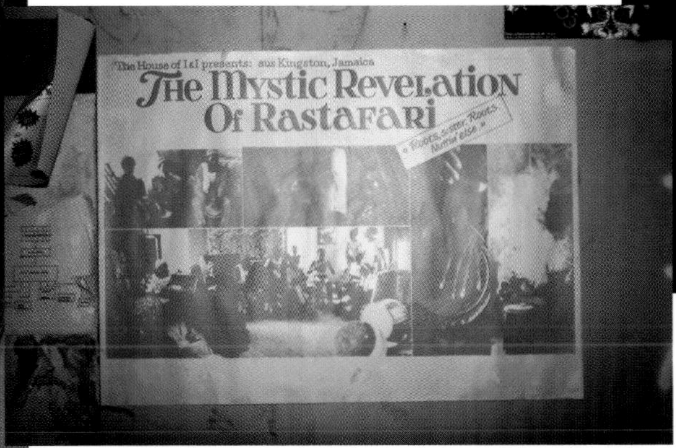

Prince Buster, when you produced the original Folkes Brothers' version of 'Oh Carolina' you used the 'buru' drums of Count Ossie, didn't you - the first time that Rastafarian musicians had been used on a Jamaican record?

Yes, and even they didn't believe it would work. It was at the studio at JBC, my first recording session, and I had to convince Ossie that, yes, it can work with just drums and not a regular band. Ossie think I take him for a fool - he call all the elders, they had seven different meetings. And when I went to the studio I'd booked, Duke Reid was in it, using it, and I fight him there, in the studio. A man named Mr Watt saw how desperate I was: he said, "Come here, Buster, forget it". He carry me upstairs and fix up a little room and bring some mikes in there and that's how 'Carolina' was made. This was the first time Rasta musicians had been used. I had to force Count Ossie to play and everybody remember it. I used to follow Ossie when I was small. I used to climb trees to follow him drums - it was always in me that I wanted to make some drums tune. Then when I had this band, a guitar, piano, drum and bass thing, that became the norm, so I look beyond it now onto the drums.

So this was basically 'nyabinghi' drumming on the record?

It is, yeah. So we took them now, carry them up a the place and set them up, give them mikes and get things going and it work. That night, you unnerstan', "no weed, mi brethren".

Left: Bernard Collins (right), and Lynford and Donald Manning, both former members of Carlton and his Shoes, made up The Abysinnians; Abysinnia, the alternative name for Ethiopia, is Arabic for 'mixed people'. The trio earned enduring legend with their tune 'Satta Massa Gana', a precursor of the gluey rhythms and minor-chord melodies of the country roots tradition that moved the Jamaican three-part harmony group away from its reliance on American soul music. Coxsone Dodd had released their equally legendary song 'Declaration Of Rights', but refused to put out 'Satta Massa Gana', considering it too radical. The group released it themselves in 1971 in their Clinch label.
Below: In the tradition of Bob Marley and Burning Spear, Culture's Joseph Hill was a mesmerising stage performer.

Lee Perry was clearly inspired by the spirit of Rastafari abroad, and it seems no coincidence that the mid-1970s were his most creative time, when he sealed his reputation with an apparently limitless series of masterful records. It was truly a golden period. When re-named simply as 'War Ina Babylon', Max Romeo's 'Sipple Out Deh' became the title track of an LP that stood out as one of the albums of the decade. The rest of the album was equally strong, especially the track 'One Step Forward', which cajoled Michael Manley for not taking a more pro-active stance against the United States. In fairness, didn't such an opinion of Manley suggest the politician was on a hiding to nothing? Attacked on the one hand by opponents who were allegedly backed by the CIA, and on the other castigated for supposedly kowtowing to Washington.

Out of the Black Ark studio there emerged in 1976 another reality song that summed up the feelings of the ghetto, 'Police And Thieves' by Junior Murvin, an anthemic song of such impact that Murvin was never able to better it. The following year it was the turn of Jah Lion's highly creative *Colombia Collie* (Lion was the name given by Scratch, ever keen to issue new sobriquets, to Jah Lloyd, a relatively established toaster on the Kingston scene). As well as a series of dub LPs, credited

to the Upsetters - such as *Cloak And Dagger*, *Revolution Dub*, and *Super Ape* - Perry voiced one of his greatest ever tunes in 'Dreadlocks In Moonlight', a haunting reggae song that bore a beautiful melody. Perry was mixing the tune one day in December 1976 when Chris Blackwell arrived to see him; when Scratch persuaded Blackwell to stay until the mix was completed, he saved the Island boss from an appointment at 56 Hope Road timed for precisely the moment when gunmen burst into the building, shooting Bob Marley.

But were any of these records as great a masterpiece as the Congos' *Heart Of The Congos* LP? The album, which was released in 1977, was an extraordinary devotional album that stands as one of the finest records ever made. An otherworldly experience, the record intertwined traditional African rhythms with Nyabinghi harmonising and sentiments, all brought to the fore by the production work of Lee 'Scratch' Perry in what was perhaps his finest work. Initially consisting of the duet of Cedric Myton and Roy Johnson, the Congos were completed, at Scratch's suggestion, by the addition of Watty Burnett.

Part of the colossal upsurge of creativity emerging from Scratch's Washington Gardens yard at that time, the group were regular features at his Black Ark studio. The Congos helped Scratch to deepen his faith in Rastafari, persuading him to grow dreadlocks, and encouraging him in the consumption of herb rather than alcohol. Scratch,

however, had fallen out with Island Records, who had hitherto been releasing much of the Black Ark material; he personally pressed up copies of their album and distributed it himself. This led to an argument between Scratch and the group. Subsequent Congos releases did not match this superlative work of art.

Culture's 'Two Sevens Clash', as epochal and enormous a hit in Jamaica in 1976 as Junior Murvin's 'Police And Thieves', was a powerful expression of prescience allied to the mysticism implicit in its numerological title: everything was about to change in 1977! The trio dealt with similar cultural and socio-political themes to Bob Marley and Burning Spear. Recorded for Joe Gibbs, the 'Two Sevens Clash' song benefited from the toppy, commercial sound that Gibbs' engineer Errol Thompson gave to everything on which he worked.

The album of the same name, also recorded for Joe Gibbs, was equally impressive - as were a number of Disco 45s for Gibbs, including 'Baldhead Bridge' and 'Forty-leg Dread'. The group was led by Joseph Hill and completed by Albert 'Ralph' Walker and Kenneth Paley; Hill proved a riveting live performer, transfixing the audience with his affliction of seriously crossed eyes. Iconically popular at the end of the 1970s, Culture enjoyed a measure of international recognition when 'Two Sevens Clash' was taken up by British punks, intrigued by Hill's apocalyptic predictions.

Signing to Virgin Records, Culture left Joe Gibbs for the seasoned and revered Kingston producer Mrs Pottinger (she had bought the Duke Reid catalogue from the late Trojan's wife), for whom they recorded the excellent *Harder Than The Rest* LP, with its 'Stop The Fighting' single.

Although the original three-piece Wailers had foundered as an operating unit, the continuing tradition of the Jamaican three-piece harmony group was not restricted to the Congos and Culture. Driven by the bass of Robbie Shakespeare and the drumming of Sly Dunbar, the Channel One 'rockers' sound, a dominant theme of reggae in the second half of the 1970s, made the Mighty Diamonds an instant hit when their commercial but highly credible *Right Time* collection was released in 1976.

Jacob Miller (top), who died in 1980 when his car crashed in Kingston's Hope Road, was the vocalist on several solo hits, including the pristine 'Cottage In Negril'; with Inner Circle, he entered the UK charts with 'Everything Is Great'. Max Romeo (centre, both photos) enjoyed success in the British charts in the summer of 1969 with his salacious 'Wet Dream'. By 1975 he was in serious 'reality' mode with his *War Ina Babylon* LP for Lee Perry. The Congos (bottom, left to right) - Watty Burnett, baritone, Cedric Myton, falsetto, and Roy Johnson, tenor - made 1977's magnificent *Heart Of The Congos* LP for Perry.

Channel One studio on Maxfield Avenue was built on the site of a former ice-cream parlour, which perhaps partially accounts for the cool sounds that emerged from it.

Owned by the four Hookim brothers (Jojo, Kenneth, Ernest and Paulie), Chinese Jamaicans who had been jukebox distributors, it opened in 1972. From 1975 onwards it rivalled Joe Gibbs' studio as a prolific centre of commercial creativity. With Ernest and Jojo most active in Channel One's output, drummer Sly Dunbar and bass-player Robbie Shakespeare, part of the house band known as the Revolutionaries, were employed to great effect on rhythms for acts like the Mighty Diamonds, developing what became known as the 'rockers' style. Often they were produced by I-Roy, who worked consistently at the studio's console.

Outside the studio, in the tough ghetto area in which it was located, half of Kingston's musicians could be found, hanging in an area that became known as 'Idler's Row', reasoning and burnin' herb.

which in Jamaica was especially acute. Cecil 'Skeleton' Spence, Albert 'Apple' Craig, and Lascelles 'Wiss' Bulgrin met up in the Mona Rehabilitation Centre on the edge of Kingston. When they espoused Rastafari and began to grow locks, however, they were kicked out of the home; they made what living they did by busking on the streets. Here they perfected the off-the-wall harmonising that by the end of 1976 propelled their tune 'Why Worry' to success; it was followed by 'The Same Song', which was also the title of their first powerful 'reality' LP. The trio came to the attention of the world following their performance supporting Bob Marley at the One Love Peace Concert in April 1978.

Out of the same Joe Gibbs studio at which Culture's 'Two Sevens Clash' was recorded came many of the classiest of cultural tunes with a pop edge, like Althea and Donna's 'Uptown Ranking', a tune that perfectly encapsulated the radical chic Manley era. Eventually the record would also become a number one national hit in the UK. The habitual studio magic employed by Gibbs' engineer Errol 'T' Thompson was employed on another hit that used the same rhythm, 'Three Piece Suit' by the deejay Trinity, whose friend Dillinger was another

The Diamonds' live debut in London at the Lyceum was only a few notches short of Bob Marley's triumph there the previous year. Signed to Virgin Records, who ill-advisedly sent the trio to New Orleans to record their next release with producer Allen Toussaint, the Diamonds' lead singer was Donald 'Tabby' Shaw, with Fitzroy 'Bunny' Simpson and Lloyd 'Judge' Ferguson largely on harmonies.

The Gladiators, meanwhile, were a militant expression of roots harmonising who came to the world's attention after they also signed to Virgin. *Trenchtown Mix-up*, their first album for the label, sounded like the expression of a fresh voice when released in 1977 - a feeling confirmed by its successors *Proverbial Reggae* and *Naturality*. In fact, the group had formed as early as 1965 and spent much of the early 1970s recording for Coxsone Dodd - for example, 'Hello Carol' on *Trenchtown Mix-up* was a 'do-over' from the Studio One era. The original version, as well as many of their other early Coxsone hits, appeared on *Presenting The Gladiators*.

Israel Vibration personified the manner in which so much Jamaican music was a triumph over adversity. In the 1950s much of the world was ravaged by a polio epidemic,

Left top: Israel Vibration, "the most cultural of groups", according to reggae expert Steve Barrow, set off their career with two classic singles, 'Why Worry' and 'The Same Song', the title of their first 'reality' LP. Left below: Dr Alimantado, the best dressed chicken in town, demonstrates that *de rigueur* Kingston footwear style of the mid-1970s - untied shoelaces. Above: The Gladiators - when in Kingston in early 1978 the author asked them what *Proverbial Reggae*, their imminent second LP for Virgin, was like, they proceeded to sing the entire set, in perfect three-part harmony. From left to right: Clinton Fearon, Dallimore Sutherland and Albert Griffiths.

significant cultural deejay; but the gruff-voiced Prince Far-I, once a bouncer at Studio One, had an even greater impact, especially with the *Cry Tuff Dub Encounter* series of records. You felt that Far-I, a live performer of staggering magnitude, really could chant down Babylon, and it was a tragedy when he was shot dead in Kingston in 1983.

After Virgin signed Prince Far-I to their Front Line label, the personable deejay had been taken up by the white rock audience. The importance of the punk-reggae fusion in Britain should not be underestimated. In his attempts at co-opting the role of sole punk archetype for himself, Sex Pistols singer John 'Rotten' Lydon claimed that he was the first person to play reggae on the radio in the UK, on a Capital Radio show broadcast on 16th July 1977. In fact, both Capital and BBC Radio London had long had their own regular reggae programmes, aimed at London's Jamaican immigrant population. Among the tunes Lydon played on this show were Augustus Pablo's 'King Tubby Meets The Rockers Uptown', Culture's 'I'm Not Ashamed', Aswad's 'Jah Wonderful', and songs by Ken Boothe, the Gladiators, and Fred Locks. But one of the records Rotten selected for this show was Dr Alimantado's 'Born For A

Purpose', a roots anthem whose popularity was assisted by the attention Rotten brought to it.

The most colourful and gregarious of the Big Youth-inspired deejays, Dr Alimantado's career had begun in 1972 with an acute identity crisis as he recorded under a different name (Winston Prince, Winston Coll and Ital Winston - Winston Thompson was his real name) each time he visited the studio. An inconsistent artist, Dr Alimantado's best work was always to be found on his own self-produced labels, Ital Sounds and Vital Food, where his wild, exuberant style of deejaying shone on tunes such as 'Plead I Cause', 'Just The Other Day', 'Poison Flour' and the Lee Perry-engineered surreal masterpiece 'The Best Dressed Chicken In Town'. Alimantado's infectious enthusiasm made him a popular character downtown where he could be found sharing his wit and wisdom with fellow musicians on North Parade. A near fatal encounter with a bus at the end of 1976 put Alimantado into Kingston's Public Hospital for six weeks: convinced that he had been spared by divine intervention, he was inspired to write 'Born For A Purpose', the record that established him as an unlikely punk-rock icon.

From St Ann's Bay came Winston Rodney, also known as Burning Spear: his gravelly vocals sounded as though they contained every piece of truth the island of Jamaica had ever known.

It was Bob Marley, another man from the parish of St Ann's, who had recommended that Rodney check the regular Sunday auditions at Studio One to see if he could get a record released. Soon Spear/Rodney had his first 45 out on Coxsone Dodd's label: 'Door Peep', another name for 'duppy', the Jamaican term for ghost, extraordinary subject-matter for a commercial disc.

By 1975, still trading under the Burning Spear name, Rodney had taken up with Rupert Wellington and Delroy Hines in a vocal trio that took the favoured Jamaican form of the three-piece harmony group to its most extreme roots. With the Ocho Rios producer Jack Ruby, Spear made the *Marcus Garvey* and *Man In The Hills* albums, remarkable poetic works that expressed the profound vision of the rural Rastafarian. Working on his own from this time onwards, Burning Spear's music swiftly developed, to the point where his 1978 LP *Social Living* had a near-jazzy timbre.

This was really revolutionary music. Spear, moreover, was an almost transcendent live performer, and his shows could touch you deep in your soul. Now based in New York, Burning Spear (pictured below left with Thomas Mapfumo, the giant of Shona music) continues to tour the world, earning the occasional Grammy, and enjoying a thoroughly deserved position as the elder statesman of reggae.

During his Capital Radio appearance, Johnny Rotten had also played *King Tubby Meets Rockers Uptown*, by the diminutive Augustus Pablo, creator of his self-named 'Far East' sound, one of the finest musicians and recording artists to come out of Jamaica. Although his greatest period was the 1970s, Pablo managed later to adapt with relative ease to computerised technology. This master of keyboards and the much maligned melodica first recorded in 1969 on a single, 'Iggy Iggy', recorded at Randy's. There, working with producer Clive Chinn, Pablo made his classic instrumental LP, *This Is Augustus Pablo*. For his own Rockers label, Pablo made *King Tubby Meets Rockers Uptown*, a magnificent dub album and one of the best records made in any field ever. 1978's *East Of The River Nile* was another instrumental set that rivalled his first release. A sickly man, the great Pablo died in 1999: with his melancholy melodica, however, he had given the roots rock era an instrumental and dub soundtrack that more than stands the test of time.

The popularity of the deejay Big Youth rivalled that of Bob Marley in Jamaica in the mid-1970s. Despite incursions into the Jamaican charts by other top deejays, more traditional solo vocalists retained their stronghold on the nation's ears. Notwithstanding the militant political and religious themes of the time, gorgeous love ditties were always present in between the most militant tunes: there seemed nothing sweeter or more tender than a Jamaican love song or singer. And none more so than Dennis Emanuel Brown, whose name was such a guarantee of vocal and recording quality during the 1970s that his sobriquet of 'The Crown Prince Of Reggae' was truly deserved. Although second only to Bob Marley in the Jamaican nation's heart, his fanbase internationally remained almost entirely within the ethnic community; his great talent was accepted as a given and it was always assumed that it was only a matter of time before he crossed over to a wider audience. Yet despite hitting the UK pop charts in 1979 with 'Money In My Pocket', Brown never greatly broadened his market.

Like many reggae performers of that era, Dennis Brown considered himself to be an 'entertainer' (such was also the case, for example, with Culture's Joseph Hill, notwithstanding his group's subject-matter of impending Armageddon). In Brown's case this reflected his background: his father was a nationally acclaimed comedian in Jamaica. "I think his father had something to do with the direction that his performances took, which were all about having a good time and a good show, not gunshots and licking people down," said Linton Kwesi Johnson, the poet and academic.

From the tough neighbourhood of Waterhouse in West Kingston came Black Uhuru, another three-piece harmony group; its most commercial incarnation was the third line-up that featured Michael Rose, Puma Jones and Ducky Simpson (left to right on opposite page). Once paired with the production talents of Sly and Robbie (background image), they produced tracks of the quality of 'Plastic Smile', 'General Penitentiary' and 'Abortion'. Signed to Island Records, Black Uhuru were pushed and promoted as a functioning live act with Sly and Robbie as honorary members; their *Sinsemilla*, *Red* and *Chill Out* albums sold strongly, and they became a sizeable concert draw - although London dates became a problem following a fatal stabbing at their London debut at the Rainbow Theatre. Their militancy may have worked against them as their career progressed into the conservative 1980s, and when first Michael Rose left the group in 1985, followed by Puma the next year, the group came to a virtual standstill - sadly, Puma Jones died of cancer in 1990.

Michael Rose: When I just begin in the music business I had to do the hotel circuit - you entertain tourists on the north coast. After I left the north coast, that's when I met Ducky. He was in Waterhouse at the time, and we link up and did some rehearsal. And then we found Puma after.

Puma: Ducky and Michael come to the gate and we just chat. Them hear I just by chance. I joined Uhuru, started to rehearse, and went to the studio, and things just step up from there.

Sly: Michael start out as a deejay, you know. But when he started singing with us, he was singing like Dennis Brown - I think he had already cut 'Guess Who's Coming To Dinner' for Niney. I could hear he had a different sound in his voice, and suggested he work at it. And when he came back about two weeks later, he started singing "*Abortion, abortion/You got to have caution*". And I said, "Wicked".

Sly: We had all these songs on tape - 'Guess Who's Coming To Dinner', 'Shine-eye Girl', 'Abortion', 'General Penitentiary' - for nine nonths, and we couldn't afford to cut a stamper. So what we do, we give U-Roy a dub-plate of all four songs. His was the only sound that had all these songs, so nobody else had it: people would go to U-Roy dance, because at four o'clock he is going to play these four Black Uhuru.

Michael: Sly and Robbie, a great combination; they play a very important part. As time goes by, as the music changes, they know the feel, and the direction of the music.

Michael Rose: It was all about to spread the message, to get the message worldwide, on issues like abortion... Growing up in a Waterhouse, man, sometimes you see some things you can,t believe. You say, "Bwai, mi can't believe them things really, really take place."

"He was very much thought of as a Peace-and-Love Rasta. But he was also one of the great child stars that reggae music produced. It's all there in the first album."

That record, *No Man Is An Island*, was released on the Studio One label in 1969, when Brown was only twelve years old: the assurance of his achingly felt vocal tone on the album's dozen songs is extraordinary for one so young, and it is hardly surprising that he became a teen sensation, sometimes described as 'the Michael Jackson of reggae'. Perhaps most important of all, his sunny personality was so engaging that the very idea of Dennis Brown would bring a smile to people's faces.

Like many Jamaican musicians, Brown had been educated at Kingston's Alpha Boys School, a kind of ghetto version of the New York City High School for the Performing Arts. As a nine-year-old he would sing with Byron Lee and the Dragonaires, often standing on beer boxes because he was so small. Following a memorable performance as the singer with the Falcon Band at a Christmas morning concert at Kingston's Carib cinema in 1968, he came to the attention of Clement 'Coxsone' Dodd, who assiduously promoted the youngster.

Just Dennis

This page: Dennis Brown, the Crown Prince of Reggae, was as big a star with the Jamaican expatriate community as Bob Marley in the late 1970s.
Opposite top: Third World, formed as a performing unit, this six-piece group's early work is still heard internationally, especially the superlative songs on *96 Degrees In The Shade*, their second LP.
Opposite below: Although Althea and Donna went quickly to the top and back to obscurity, this pair of schoolgirls made one of the best pop singles of all time with the Joe Gibbs' produced 'OEUptown Top Ranking'.

Delgado. But it was his work for the producers Joe Gibbs and Winston 'Niney' Holness for which he was best known. For Gibbs Brown recorded great cultural hits like 'Cup Of Tea' and 'Slave Driver', and at the end of the 1970s three outstanding albums - *Visions*, *Words Of Wisdom*, and *Joseph's Coat Of Many Colours*. Although Gibbs had produced 'Money In My Pocket, in 1972, Brown recorded it a second time for Niney in 1978, the hit version. The raw rhythms that were Niney's special flavour pushed Brown's extraordinary voice to peaks of creative excellence. 'Wolf And Leopard' was another especially creative endorsement of their collaboration - it became the title-track of a 1977 album that was something of a benchmark for the roots era. "Even today that always raises a cheer in a blues dance," said Linton Kwesi Johnson. "That song, which is essentially an anthem to black people, is so radical you feel it should have been a Bob Marley tune," commented Don Letts, the Rastafarian film director. "It shows the full extent to which Dennis could deliver songs with incredible messages. Yet he ended up succumbing to the wolves."

Dennis Brown had the facility to step between the sweetest, most heart-tugging romantic laments and serious Rastafarian cultural themes. "He embodied the joyous spirit of the golden age of conscious reggae, a life-affirming presence in the flesh and on wax who made your day a little bit better when you saw him," said the writer Vivien Goldman.

Although he wrote many of his own songs, Brown was also a great interpreter of other writers' material - one of his most acclaimed covers being his version of Peter Green's 'Black Magic Woman' for the producer Phil Pratt. For his own DEB label, Brown recorded a stream of tunes, as well as producing artists of the calibre of Junior

The 'wolves' in question were those of the scourge of cocaine that increasingly began to blight Jamaica from the late 1970s and was one of the causes of Brown's death in 1999. So impressive were the cunning abilities of Jamaica's ganja smugglers that they found themselves sought out by Colombian cocaine cartels. The cultural ramifications of this linger to this day, both in the UK and USA, where from the mid-1980s Jamaican gangs set up street-level dealing of crack cocaine, and on the island itself, where the shift to the rougher sound of dancehall has been attributed to the effects of cocaine instead of ganja.

Another fabulous talent whose upward career trajectory altered course in a direct response to his cocaine consumption was the once masterly Gregory Isaacs - Gregory, the original 'Cool Ruler', could have been a champion on a close-to-Bob Marley scale. Isaac's sweet crooning voice was the languid weapon of seduction of this honorary king of lover's rock; his personal Golden Age fell in the later half of the 1970s: "He was the number one singer in the reggae world in the period 1977-1979," says historian Steve Barrow.

Hardly a week seemed to go by without yet another Gregory single being released - new albums came every month or so - all absolutely top quality. The man was formidably prolific: a 1978 album, released by GG, entitled *The Best Of Gregory Isaacs* suggested an LP of recent hits - instead, it was an immensely strong record of fresh tunes, recorded at Channel One, featuring the Revolutionaries. Not long after, *The Best Of Gregory Isaacs, Volume 2* appeared, from the same source.

Gregory could have been a real contender, the man whose visits to the Cecil Gee store seemingly kept the UK clothing chain in profit had the most heartfelt style you could hope to hear. An enormous talent, he could pen a deliciously sensual song at the drop of one of his broad-brimmed hats; even at the turn of the millennium, a new Gregory Isaacs tune was still a guarantee of some quality.

"Gregory Isaacs is Kingstonian, y'know. Born and raised in the ghetto, man. So somewhere along the line we know the two, even out of the music. Gregory Isaacs is a great believer, and a man that could see things." BIG YOUTH

From a desperately poor rural background in Davey Town in inland Manchester, Jepther McClymont took his *nom de disque* from the surname of the ruthless Mafia enforcer Lucky Luciano. It is almost surprising, then, that in the mid-1990s he became Jamaica's king of consciousness, his addictive records seemingly never off the Jamaican radio airwaves.

"It seems," says Luciano, offering an explanation, in humility, "that of late consciousness in mankind has raised up to a higher dimension. For some reason myself and other artists began to feel a need to ameliorate the subconscious human condition down here in Jamaica: we realised the impact that music has on young minds."

Moving to Kingston, Luciano at first had worked as an upholsterer before being beaten back by the hustle of the city. Moving to Montego Bay, he became an orange-seller, before returning to Kingston and recording for Sky High, Castro Brown and Freddie McGregor. Working with the renowned Phillip 'Fatis' Burrell on his Xterminator label, Luciano moved increasingly in a 'conscious' direction. *Where There Is Life*, his second Fatis-produced set, was a beautiful work of great maturity and thought, including gorgeous songs like 'How Can You' ("*How can you be so ungrateful/After all that God has done for you...*"), many of which have a distinct country and western feel. His other Fatis-produced records, *One Way Ticket* and *The Messenger*, are of an almost equal standard. Although he no longer works with Fatis, Luciano regularly tours internationally: although his live performances sometimes tend towards histrionics, they are always uplifting experiences.

Who are you, Luciano?

I see myself as a serious messenger of the Almighty Jah,
who has come to teach mankind something. We have all had our rough times in life, and after learning I and I realise what must be done. So for the benefit of our youngsters, and to redeem old souls, I must do things to spread the positive energy in life: by uniting with I and I it is the same Rastafari fire, igniting within I and I until we can continue to lift the flame higher and higher. Until you never know where we can lift it to. If allowed I and I can take the fire so high that mankind tremble in the sight of Jah Rastafari.

When did you learn that you must find yourself to pursue your course?

You cannot join in until you find yourself.
It's not like going to look for a brother down there who has the good herb. It's about looking, studying new philosophies, putting them to work until you can see how good they work. Until you can see how better you can make your community and your environment: how you can create a better world, and make people see that love is the only essence by which I and I can survive and live.

Because over the years you've tested and you've proved
and you can see that if you do bad, bad follow you, and if you do good, good follow you. So from there, you start to build your own philosophies and search and search deeper and deeper until you can see how well you can come out, how better you can express your soul. So it's a constant search as long as life goes on: I and I will always be searching I and I's soul. Because if there is no depth and no heights, I and I have to have boundaries for I and I to manipulate and use to the glory of the Almighty Jah who worketh in I and I for iver and iver. Jah Rastafari, Selassie-I.

But all the same, you are a great role model...

Well, it boils down to discipline. And kingciple.
It boils down to knowing that your brother is a part of you, and you should love your brother as yourself, and the Almighty with all your heart. And even though we have unravelled a certain part of our consciousness, we still know that there is

"I think Luciano is reminding me of Bob Marley right now - because Luciano is really great". LADY SAW

confusion around the world. In the Rastafarian movement, you have, some say, Twelve Tribes, Nyabinghi, Bobashanti, some Orthodox, some just natural true seekers. I and I see I-self as everyone self, ca' it all follow under the umbrella of Rastafari.

As we say 'Emperor Haile Selassie-I',

we automatically become a part of his kingdom. And we should all be proud to associate ourselves as Africans and as black people who have found existence to be a spiritual phenomenon. We have to be happy to cling to our heritage - that is our roots, and if we deny our roots then we deny our own soul, and we deny ourselves, and we deny our own presence and existence.

Someone said to me that they love Luciano because he acknowledges the existence of all philosophies.

At the end of the day one has to know who Luciano is. Because he is not

just a singer who people come and dance to. I want them to love I for the life that I lead and the righteousness that I try to give in my music. And by that you can move to a better calling, and clean up your act. And make this world a better world, because you know that there is hypocrisy going on. And I and I don't dig that.

Hasn't there always been a duality in Jamaican music: the rude boy on one side and the spiritual on the other?

I say there has been a segregation and a separation ever since the creation of man. So what you see happening is

just a display coming out in the music. And you see it in the factories, how people build things and try to compete: even that is a part of it.

It boils down to love still, because at the

end of the day you realise that love is just principle, love is kingciple, love is righteous, love is everything. And to have that unconditional love, there has to be justice. At the end of the day to survive in this system we must just exercise the principles of life. Especially those that claim they want to lead and rule the world. They must follow the principles of Emperor Haile Selassie I.

Tell me the importance of herb in Jamaica and Rastafari.

Herb is unto I and I, as the living words is

to my meditation.

And on a more secular level, the importance of country and Western music in Jamaica.

The more universal you become in the mind, the less boundaries you put to music. You realise that everyone

who is dancing somehow, whether to salsa, or funk, or to Nyabinghi, has a rightful place in existence. And I say, if allowed to see a brighter light, everyone of us can move to a more universal calling. And I say that is what we are here about, to spread the universalness in the music.

Just to bring across the message:

sometimes we say 'Lord', sometimes we say 'God', or 'Jesus', or 'Father' - words with which people are already associated, so we can touch the depths of their meditation, and instigate some improvement in their mind and in their soul. So that's what it is all about.

We will compromise at times, just to

allow the flow of the word until we reach another level of consciousness. Jah is full of inspiration, and subtleness; Jah is full of uniqueness, so we have to know that Jah will not move like politicians move.

You've had great success and have travelled a lot. How do you feel your life has changed?

I tell you the honest truth, my brother, when you get bigger, a whole heap of things

gwan. But I tell you, if I was to view life from a materialistic point of view, I would say my life mash up. But being a man of understanding, I know that what is happening is a spiritual thing. I realise that even in my own family, you have seen that the judgement have hit. So I say, at this stage I have to be even stronger and more militant in I and I's philosophies to keep this temple, because I know there is a knowledge within that anyone who is willing to listen to I and I can lift their own meditation to a higher level to find his songs and find his energy to do things.

What happens to people is that over the

years, they become too lazy, because of the revolutionary activities of the industry, which turns people into zombies, a living death: the things they should be elevating and propagating now in life, they fight.

This is the final call: the system is going down.

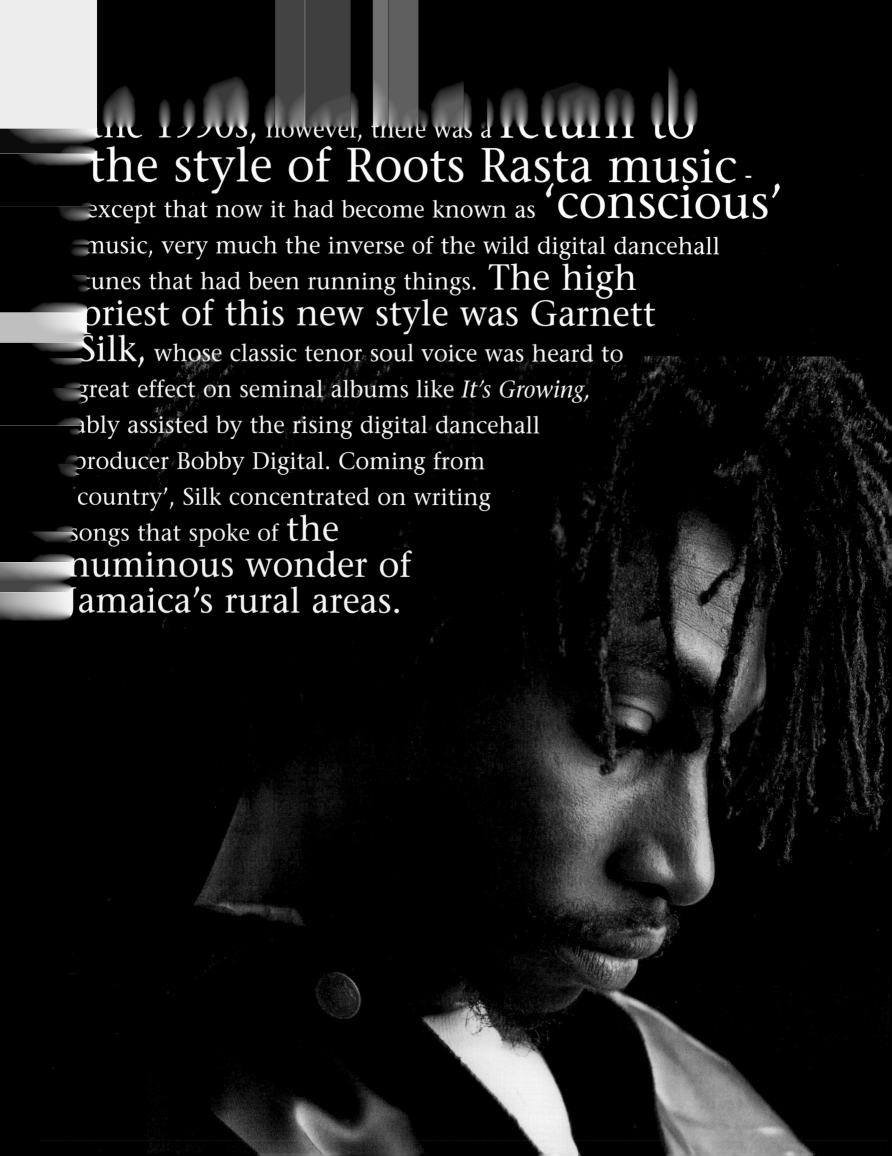

the 1990s, however, there was a return to the style of Roots Rasta music – except that now it had become known as 'conscious' music, very much the inverse of the wild digital dancehall tunes that had been running things. The high priest of this new style was Garnett Silk, whose classic tenor soul voice was heard to great effect on seminal albums like *It's Growing,* ably assisted by the rising digital dancehall producer Bobby Digital. Coming from 'country', Silk concentrated on writing songs that spoke of the numinous wonder of Jamaica's rural areas.

Silk, Sizzla, Buju. As the man who overtly brought consciousness into dancehall, the position of Garnett Silk (opposite) in the pantheon of Jamaican music is assured. Sizzla (left), who desires to come to England "to talk to Elizabeth 'bout repatriation", is the Bobbadread deejay star, courtesy of such excellent tunes as 'Black Woman And Child', as well as riveting live performances. Thanks to his epochal *Til Shiloh* set, Buju Banton (right) has developed into a conscious archetype.

Gregory Isaacs always possessed the capability to be a huge international cross-over artist. But his predilection for the badman life put an end to that - even by the time he recorded his almost-crossover classic 'Night Nurse' in 1982, his career was already on a downswing.

Following the death of Bob Marley in 1981, reggae and Rastafari no longer seemed interlinked: dancehall styles predominated and there was less specific reference in songs to Jah. Yet even in the slackest of tunes, there was often an undercurrent of Rastafarian religiosity that had come to be taken as a given. On the other hand there were artists like Cocoa Tea, a devout dreadlocked Rasta who cut plenty of records informed by his faith. A sweet-voiced singer associated with the first burst of raw dancehall records of the early 1980s, Cocoa Tea had emerged from the same sound system circuits as the new breed of deejays, and was adept at similar microphone improvisations. Working with Jammy, Gussie Clarke and Junjo Lawes among others, he cut a niche for himself that was still there at the end of the century.

Johnny Osbourne similarly had established his niche as a major artist right at the beginning of that decade with his *Truths And Rights* LP for Studio One. A masterly, understated set, it is a classic album. One of the most popular singers in Jamaica at the time, this major artist had a huge success in 1983 with 'Water Pumping', and the hits continued throughout the decade.

After Garnett Silk's accidental death in a house fire in 1994, Luciano, a hitmaker with a substantial supply of his own addictive spiritual songs, seized Silk's mantle. Some of the most exemplary 'conscious' music came from older dancehall acts who had experienced Biblical-like conversions - like Capleton, a raucous dancehall deejay who changed his style and became associated with the same Bobbadread posse as Sizzla. None was more remarkable than Buju Banton, once the personification of Jamaican homophobia. But after he grew dreadlocks, Banton produced the finest reggae album of the 1990s - *Til Shiloh*, a work of mature spirituality.

"In the same way that the music has changed, so there will also be a breaking down of this present world order," predicted Luciano, at the dawn of a new millennium. "Even world leaders know this current system is collapsing. Any system that isn't based on equality and justice simply cannot last."

It was a point with which Bob Marley, who had pioneered international acceptance of this vein of Jamaican thought, would have unequivocally agreed.

The baby boy was born

at around 2.30 on the Wednesday morning of 6th February 1945. He weighed seven pounds, four ounces, and the name he was given was **Nesta Robert Marley,** the Robert at the request of Norval, his white father. At the age of five Nesta was taken away from his birthplace of Nine Miles

THE MARLEY

in the parish of St Ann's by his father: they moved to Kingston, where his father to all intents and purposes deserted him, placing his son in the care of a woman who lived downtown. After a year **Cedella, his mother,** discovered where Nesta was living and brought him back from Kingston. Before his sojourn in the capital, **Nesta had displayed a gift as a palmreader.**

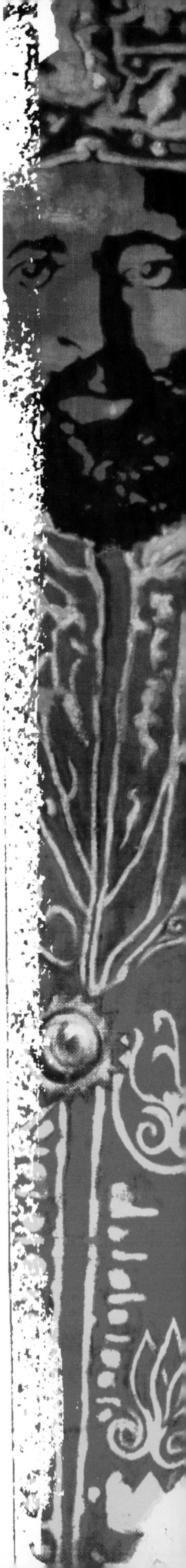

When a woman back at Nine Miles asked the boy to read her hand, he shook his head. "No," said Nesta, "I'm not reading no more hand: I'm singing now." "He had these two little sticks," Cedella recalls. "He started knocking them with his fists in this rhythmical way and singing this old

LEGACY

Jamaican song: *'Hey Mr, won't you touch me potato/Touch me yam, punking tomato/All you do is King Love, King Love/Ain't you tired of squeeze up, squeeze up/Hey Mr, won't you touch me potato/Touch me yam, punking potato.'* "And it just made the woman feel so good, and she gave him two or three pennies. That was the first time he talked about music." Soon after, Cedella herself moved to Kingston, returning to see her son at weekends.

When Nesta was twelve, Cedella decided it was time for him to come and live with her in Kingston. She moved to 19 Second Street in Trench Town, where he osmosed the moods, and more, of an area defined as a ghetto. One of his closest friends was a youth called Bunny Livingston, with whose father Cedella had had an affair.

It was in the yard of an esteemed local musician called Joe Higgs that Nesta first encountered something that stilled his thoughts sufficiently to empathise with the lateral processes of jazz, a genre favoured by Higgs. "After a while I smoke some ganja, some herb, and get to understand it. Me try to get into de mood whar de moon is blue and see de feelin' expressed. Joe Higgs 'elped me understand that music. 'E taught me many t'ings."

Another of the male role models who appeared throughout the course of the fatherless Nesta's life, Joe Higgs assiduously coached the 15-year-old and his spar Bunny in the art of harmonising: he would advise Bob to sing all the time, to strengthen his voice. At one of these sessions Bob and Bunny met Peter McIntosh, another youth wanting to 'mek a try' as a vocalist, who lived in nearby West Road.

At the urging of Joe Higgs, they formed into a musical unit: the Teenagers contained the three youths, as well as a strong local singer called Junior Braithwaite and two girls who sang backing vocals, Beverley Kelso and Cherry Smith. The Teenagers became first the Wailing Rudeboys, and then the Wailing Wailers.

A 'brethren' of Higgs, Alvin 'Franseeco' Patterson (later known simply as Seeco) instructed the prospective musicians in the philosophy of rhythm. Seeco was another professional musician now living in Trench Town: the burru style of drumming he played was an African rhythm of liberation, co-opted into Rastafari's Nyabinghi style of inspirational chanting and drum-rhythms. It was this blend of devotion and rebellious fervour that formed the basis of the Wailers' understanding of rhythm.

Above: Bob and Rita and their children - from left, Bob's step-daughter Sharon, Ziggy and Cedella; seated in the pushchair is Steven. Right: Ziggy and Rita.

After meeting Derrick Morgan, Nesta, who now called himself Bob, linked up with producer Leslie Kong and made his first record. 'Judge Not' was recorded at Federal Studios in August 1962, the same month that Jamaica gained independence - the shrill, youthful voice of Bob Marley had the joyous gallop of ska as the backbeat to his first recorded work. But the celebratory sound of 'Judge Not' could not conceal the Biblical tone that was significantly present in his first release: chiding those who pass judgement on himself and his kind, he warns that *'While you talk about me/Someone else is judging you'*.

Released under the name of 'Robert Marley', the song sold hardly at all and radio plays were non-existent.

Two other Bob Marley ska numbers, 'Terror' and 'One Cup Of Coffee', were put out by Kong as 45s, to little avail. The few listeners assumed it was the work of one 'Bobby Martell': Kong had renamed Bob with this kitsch moniker in much the same way as he changed James Chambers to Jimmy Cliff.

Despite this lack of success, the 16-year-old Bob Marley had decided to make a serious go of it with his spars from Trench Town. Seeco was acquainted with Clement 'Coxsone' Dodd, the sound system man who had begun his own record label. Seeco knew of the auditions that Coxsone would regularly hold on Sundays at Studio One, his new one-track studio on Brentford Road, to the north of Trench Town. Shortly before Christmas 1963, at the urging of Joe Higgs, Seeco took Bob and the rest of the group, including Beverley Kelso and Cherry Smith, over there.

Listening to them in his studio's dusty yard, beneath the mango tree that was the location of these weekly auditions, Coxsone liked their sound and several of the songs they had written. They were offered Coxsone's standard deal: a five-year contract for exclusive recording rights and management, and a guarantee of twenty pounds a side. The first session took place within days; the sides selected for recording were 'I'm Still Waiting' and 'It Hurts To Be Alone'.

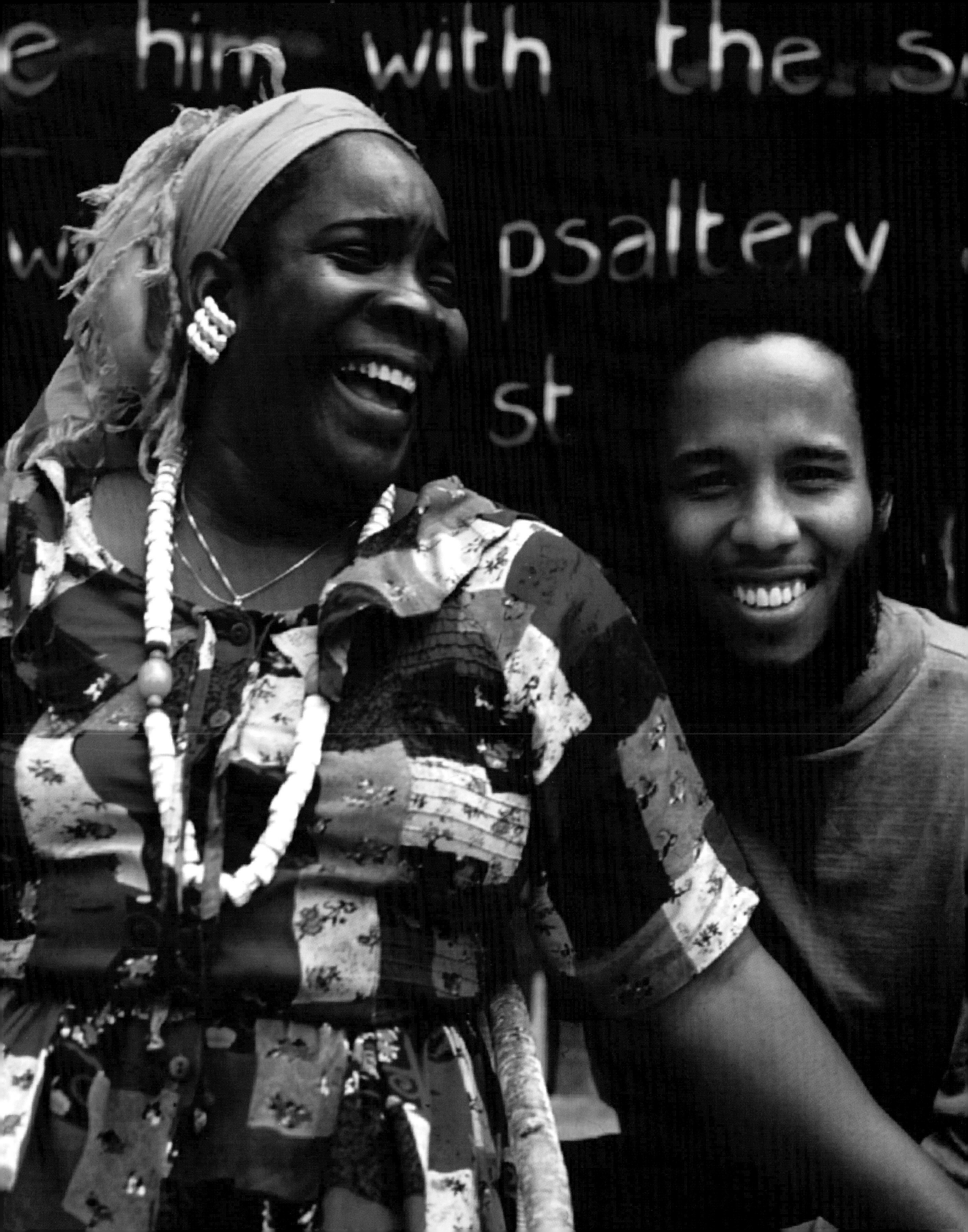
him with the
psaltery
st

'I'm Still Waiting' was a beautiful Bob Marley original, even though the preamble of the vocal harmonies owed much to the Impressions. But when Bob delivered his breathtakingly sweet vocal solo, it bled from a tearful heart. Suspended in a void of echoing pain, his voice felt as though it had been recorded at a different, slowed-down speed compared to the rest of the track. 'It Hurts To Be Alone' was a Junior Braithwaite number on which he sang lead. As Coxsone's house arranger, Ernest Ranglin oversaw the production of the pair of sides. As soon as Coxsone heard this, he called the group back to the studio. If he was to continue working with the group, Coxsone insisted, the Wailers required a clearly defined lead vocalist.

It was decided that the task should fall to Bob; Bunny and Peter were promised they would also get their share of lead vocals.

"My greatest influence in early times was the Drifters - 'Magic Moment', 'Please Stay', those things. So I figured I should get a group together."

BOB MARLEY

Right: The Wailers, with their gold lamé Beatle jackets - from left to right, Bob, Bunny Livingston and Peter Tosh, with Beverley Kelso. Left: Bob used to return to Nine Miles half a dozen times a year: it would be his final resting place (above).

Coxsone was encouraged in the decision to choose a lead vocalist for the Wailers by 'Simmer Down', a song Bob had brought to the session that served a dual purpose: a warning to the newly emergent rude boys not to bring down the wrath of the law upon themselves; and a frustrated response to a letter from his mother who was living in the United States, fearful that her only son was becoming involved with bad company.

The full panoply of his label's finest ska musicians was summoned by Coxsone for the session. Yet again Ernest Ranglin arranged the tune, whilst Don Drummond, Jamaica's master of the trombone, added his deeply creative jazz parts.

Bob Marley live at the studio and sleep in a back room they'd use for auditions or rehearsals. Bob was unable to put his head down, however, until the sessions had ended, often late into the night.

In 1967 Bob revealed to the other Wailers that he intended to set up his own operation, the Wail'N'Soul'M record store, in honour of its first two acts, the Wailers and the Soulettes, the group that included Rita, his new wife. To this effect Bob installed a counter window in their little home, as it reverted to by night. A first single was released, 'Bend Down Low', recorded at Studio One but produced by Bob and put out on his own label. 'Mellow Mood', the B-side, was one of Bob's finest songs ever.

By now Bob was also learning some good lessons himself. A number of the musicians playing at Studio One were dedicated and devout Rastafarians. For years Bob's Bible had rarely been out of his sight. Now he began to be offered new interpretations that would make his jaw drop with disbelief.

For the rest of 1964 the Wailing Wailers were rarely out of the Jamaican charts, with a string of tunes recorded at 13 Brentford Road: 'Lonesome Feeling', 'Mr Talkative', 'I Don't Need Your Love', 'Donna', 'Wings Of A Dove'. 'Mr Dodd' became another father figure to Bob, and, to a lesser extent, to Bunny and Peter. When he learned that Bob had no home of his own, Coxsone did a deal with the youth. He would turn new artists over to Bob to find songs for them; Bob could then take his guitar and sit down - with Delroy Wilson or Hortense Ellis, for example - and rehearse the tune. In return, Clement Dodd would let

Mortimer Planner, the dread who had led Haile Selassie down the steps of his plane onto the tarmac at Kingston airport, had become a sort of combination of mentor and manager to Bob. Planner had encountered Danny Sims, an American living in Jamaica. Sims, who promoted concerts throughout the Caribbean, managed Johnny Nash, a handsome Texan-born singer with a sweet, powerful voice who had also moved to Kingston, and was probably the first international artist to co-opt Jamaican rhythms into his tunes.

When Sims got in touch with Bob, the musician sent Planner along to negotiate. After Planner and Sims had had "a few lickle rough talks", the American ended up addressing the dread as "chief" and an agreement was struck. Impressed with Bob's songwriting skills, Sims committed himself to breaking Bob both as a songwriter and as an artist in his own right.

Peter Tosh was born in 1944 in Grange Hill, Westmoreland. Moving from Savanna-La-Mar to Denham and then Trench Town as a boy, Tosh had already become a competent guitarist, owning his own cheap acoustic model. By the time he met Bob Marley and Bunny Livingston his skill on the instrument inspired Bob to seriously master the guitar. Whilst Bob Marley was in the USA in 1966 Tosh recorded 'I'm The Toughest' and 'Rasta Shook Them Up'; for Scratch Perry he recorded 'Second Hand' and 'Downpresser'. And before the Wailers split, Tosh had already formed his Intel Diplo H.I.M. (Intelligent Diplomat for His Imperial Majesty) label. For Intel Diplo he recorded such classics as 'Stepping Razor' and 'Legalise It', a plea for tolerance over herb, for which he was busted several times, being savagely beaten on more than one occasion. His later recordings for the Rolling Stones label were curiously patchy - though he hit with a cover of the Temptations' 'Don't Look Back'. Tosh's talent was almost outweighed by an all consuming bitterness: he could seem like the personification of Bob Marley's shadow - an erratic, enormously gifted man, his pain was an equal with that of Bob. But both were bound together by a natural rebellion against what Tosh defined as the "shit-stem". Peter Tosh was no stranger to tragedy, which included an awkward childhood. His legendary prickliness intensified after he wrote off his car in 1973 in a crash that killed his then girlfriend and in which Tosh suffered severe skull fractures. On 11th September 1987, Peter Tosh was gunned down in a home invasion at his house in Kingston.

"Peter was always difficult. I found Bunny easier than him, because Bunny was consistently 'no', he didn't want to tour overseas, didn't want to have anything to do with Babylon. Peter was yes and then no, yes and then no." CHRIS BLACKWELL

Marley's deal with Danny Sims was that Bob would receive adequate royalties for his songwriting and a publishing deal with Sims' company, Cayman Music; the Wailers would each be put on a retainer of 50 US dollars a week.

In addition the Wailers soon linked up with Lee 'Scratch' Perry: the recordings that resulted were the finest work done by both parties. Scratch persuaded them to drop their doo-wop harmonising and follow the innate feel of the sound within their own heads, literally to find their own voices. The first song that the Wailers, Scratch, and his studio musicians the Upsetters recorded together, at Randy's Studio in the downtown section known as Parade, was 'My Cup', quickly followed by 'Duppy Conqueror', in which the Wailers proclaimed that if any bad forces came along to test them, they could just mash them down with their spiritual strength and power. Numerous singles emerged from several inspirational sessions, and the songs were packaged by Scratch into a pair of LPs, *Soul Rebels* and *Soul Revolution*.

Meanwhile, with the help of Alan 'Skill' Cole, Jamaica's leading footballer and a close friend of Bob, the group formed their own label, Tuff Gong, in the summer of 1971. The first tune released was called 'Trench Town Rock', a song about suffering, and the life lived in Trench Town: despite the disadvantaged environs in which they found themselves, Bob and Rita and the Wailers would sit out at night making music "*and when it hit you feel no pain*".

"We were classed as ghetto people, but we knew that our time would come, because we were sowing good seed," said Rita. The group's time did come, almost immediately this record was released: it stayed at number one for much of the summer. On their own label the Wailers were finally on top of the charts, their rightful position; at last they would earn some good amounts of cash from their own efforts.

Then Danny Sims asked Bob if he would fly over to Stockholm, where Johnny Nash was starring in a film called *Love Is Not A Game*. Could Bob write some songs for the soundtrack? But although Bob went to Scandinavia, he had a miserable experience; when he moved down to London, a promised support tour with Nash failed to materialise - though Bob played guitar in a group that backed Nash on some dates in English secondary schools; CBS, meanwhile, singularly failed to promote 'Reggae On Broadway', a Bob Marley solo single.

Bob made a decision. There was, as far as he could make out, to be only one avenue of escape. He arranged for Brent Clarke, a record company promotions man of Jamaican origin who did work for Sims, to effect an introduction with Chris Blackwell, the founder of Britain's most successful independent record company, Island Records.

Bunny Livingston became re-branded as Bunny Wailer following the break-up of the original group. As soon as his *Blackheart Man* album was released in 1976, it was apparent that as a solo artist Bunny was a very large talent indeed.

As a teenager in Jamaica, Chris Blackwell had been on a boat that ran aground in shallow waters; after a long and exhausting swim to the shore, he collapsed on a beach where he was picked up and carried to a Rastafarian encampment; its inhabitants cared for his wounds, and fed him with both 'ital' food and rhetoric from the philosophy of Rastafari. The white Jamaican would never be the same again.

In 1958, at the age of 21, Blackwell started a small record label in Kingston. Producing the records himself, he gave the label the name Island Records. Blackwell first hit the Jamaican charts in 1959 with Laurel Aitken and the tune 'Boogie In My Bones'; the record made the Cuban-born Aitken, who had emulated the style of the Memphis bluesman Roscoe Gordon, the biggest star in Jamaica. With the proceeds Chris Blackwell set up shop in a small office on South Odeon Avenue in midtown Kingston's thronging commercial suburb of Half Way Tree.

In 1961, the first James Bond movie, *Dr No*, was filmed on location in Jamaica. Drawing on his local expertise, producer Harry Saltzman made Blackwell his production assistant. When the film, destined to be enormously successful, wrapped, Saltzman offered him a more permanent position. Torn between the two paths diverging before him, Chris Blackwell took advice from a local seer, a Lebanese woman. His future was clear to her: he should stick with the record business, she said. The next year he moved his operations to London.

On his way to begin his record company in London, Blackwell stopped off in New York. There he had lunch with Ahmet Ertegun, who was the owner of Atlantic Records: Chris Blackwell's approach to the record business had been influenced by his observations of the way that black talent was nurtured at Atlantic. "I think Chris may be a little more adventurous than me, a little more avant-garde," was the conclusion at which Ertegun was eventually to arrive.

Having made licensing agreements with the leading Jamaican producers to release their product in the UK,

Chris Blackwell was in tune with the spirit and the ideals of Rastafari far more than the vast majority of other white Jamaicans. Opposite page, bottom left: With Jacob Miller and Inner Circle.

Chris Blackwell aimed his releases at Britain's West Indian immigrant community; one of the first records he put out was a tune from Leslie Kong, 'Judge Not' by Robert Marley: the surname was mis-spelt as 'Morley' on the British release.

Two years later Millie Small, a Jamaican singer he was managing, had a huge worldwide hit with 'My Boy Lollipop'. After that Chris Blackwell was drawn into the world of pop and rock: he managed the Spencer Davis Group, which featured Steve Winwood, and launched Island as a rock label on the back of Winwood's Traffic. Soon Island became the most sought-after label for groups specialising in the underground rock of the late 1960s.

After taking on the management of Jimmy Cliff, the successful Jamaican singer, Blackwell observed with pleasure the prospect of marketing the sexy rebel image that Cliff portrayed in the ground-breaking movie *The Harder They Come*. But then Cliff decided to leave Island, precisely because he thought the label was becoming too rock-orientated. Just at that point Bob Marley re-entered Blackwell's life.

Although he had released Marley's first single, Blackwell had hardly kept track of his career. All he knew was that he had been warned about the Wailers, that these guys were 'trouble'. "But in my experience when people are described like that, it usually just means that they know what they want."

The Island boss cut a deal with Bob Marley and the group. He would give them £4,000 to return to Jamaica and make an LP. When he received the final tapes they would get another £4,000. He also agreed to give Tuff Gong the rights to Wailers material in the Caribbean, which was to provide a useful source of ready cash in the coming years. (A deal also had to be struck with Danny Sims: for another £4,000 Blackwell bought Bob out of his contract with CBS.) "Everyone told me I was mad: they said I'd never see the money again." Blackwell ignored these naysayers. And he proffered advice as to how he believed the career of the three singers should be pursued. The idea of a vocal trio with backing musicians was dated, he told them: they should take their favourite musicians and forge themselves into a tight road band, capable of touring and presenting several layers of identity in addition to the one surrounding Bob Marley.

"Here was this Third World superstar emerging, an individual against the system with an incredible look: this was the first time you had seen anyone looking like that, other than Jimi Hendrix. And Bob had that power about him and incredible lyrics."

On their return to Jamaica, the group immediately went into Harry J's studio in Kingston. By the end of the year, following further sessions at Dynamic and Randy's, the album, which was to be called *Catch A Fire*, had been completed. Chris Blackwell set about marketing the record.

A decision was made that *Catch A Fire* should be the first reggae album sold as though it was by a rock act. In line with Blackwell's thinking, rock guitar and keyboards were added to the LP at Island's Basing Street studio in London's Notting Hill. Then the cover was worked on, an outsize cardboard replica of a Zippo cigarette lighter. It hinged upwards and the record was removed from the top of the sleeve - in fact, the discs often stuck within the packaging, but the desired effect was created all the same.

"What Bob Marley believed in and how he lived his life was something that had tremendous appeal for the press," said Chris Blackwell. "The press had been dealing with the greatest time in the emergence of rock'n'roll and it was starting to quieten down."

When *Catch A Fire* was released in Britain, in December 1972, it was pitched at the very hippest sections of the media. In London the next Spring the Wailers were slotted in for four nights at The Speakeasy, a long fashionable, somewhat elitist club catering largely to musicians and the music business. Such was the buzz created by *Catch A Fire* that this set of London shows was a complete sell-out.

Immediately the group was a critical success, although a commercial breakthrough was still some way off. Returning to Jamaica, the Wailers quickly recorded *Burnin'*, their second album for Island Records. For *Catch A Fire* Bob had gone up to London on his own to supervise the overdubbing of certain guitar parts that gave the LP more of a 'rock' feel. This time, however, all the Wailers went to the Island studios in Basing Street, Notting Hill. When Chris Blackwell showed them the two studios, they opted for the smaller one, down in the basement of the building, which reminded Family Man Barrett of the Treasure Isle studios in Kingston.

"We say, 'This is the one: feel the beat.' You can really feel the bottom." In the middle of November the Wailers returned to England for their second tour that year. The weather was bitterly cold, and for the first dates the group had been booked into a series of shows in colleges in the grimmest industrial cities in the north of England. However, they only played a total of four dates out of the 26 that had been booked.

After an almost mournful performance at Leeds Polytechnic, the group set out to drive the 200 miles back to London. The next show was in Northampton, on 30th November. As they arrived at the venue thick snow was falling. Bunny and Peter, who argued violently with Bob, interpreted this as a clear sign that the tour was doomed, a view which Bunny announced in the exaggeratedly precise BBC English with which he would consider only the very most important of issues. By abandoning the dates and boarding a flight back to Jamaica, they turned this perception into a self-fulfilling prophecy. Soon the other two founder members had officially left the group. Now it really was Bob Marley and the Wailers.

At the end of 1974 Bob went out to stay for a few days with Lee Perry at his home in Cardiff Crescent in the Washington Gardens section of Kingston. "We were all of us talking, talking, and Bob said, 'Bwai, mi not know what fe do'," said Perry's wife Pauline, who as a girl would see Bob singing under the tree in Trench Town on her way home from school. "So I said to him how American artists would all have a very identifiable set of people to work with. And if you have three girls with you, you will look representative of the way people are performing in foreign. Bob laugh and say, "Which three girls?" - "I say to him, 'You have Marcia Griffiths, you have Judy Mowatt, and you have Rita, your wife'. He said to me, 'Them girls, deh?' Mi say, 'Of course, because those are the three girls mi really see now could go fe back up a man like you'. 'Im say, 'OK, mi see how it go'."

The next album *Natty Dread* (retitled from *Knotty Dread*), was released to great critical acclaim. Credited for the first time to Bob Marley and the Wailers, the record had also registered far higher sales figures than either of the Wailers' two previous Island albums. To continue the record's promotion, an American tour was set up, followed by a brief foray into the English market (two London shows, one in Birmingham, one in Manchester) and - for the first time ever - some European dates.

"The *Natty Dread* album," said Bob, "is like one step more forwards for reggae music. Better music, better lyric, it have a better feelin'. *Catch A Fire* and *Burnin'* have a good feelin', but *Natty Dread* is improved."

Both of the London shows at the Lyceum were recorded for a live album. A spiky concert version of the tune 'No Woman No Cry', featured on the *Natty Dread* album, was put out as a single. It was a Top Ten hit, Bob Marley's first chart single, and the live album also charted.

In May of the next year these first signs of chart success were followed by another album - *Rastaman Vibration*, a consummately satisfying work that concluded with 'War', a song whose lyrics were taken from a speech that Haile Selassie had made to the United Nations. The record was the first international long-playing hit by Bob Marley, all-importantly making the US Top Ten. Its release was followed by a European and US tour that simply cemented Bob's status.

Jamaicans are never ones to genuflect to status, however and this became only too apparent at the end of the year. Bob agreed to play the 'Smile Jamaica' concert, scheduled for 5th December 1976 at Kingston's National Heroes Park.

At first Chris Blackwell had advised against the show, which initially was to take place in the grounds of Jamaica House: what Bob told him about the proposed show suggested it was to be billed as a PNP event.

Bob Marley went back to Michael Manley, and was assured that this was the last thing the Prime Minister wanted; Bob was being invited to the event by the government of Jamaica and therefore would perform for the entire nation: the 'Smile Jamaica' poster was to contain the wording "Concert presented by Bob Marley in association with the Cultural Department of the Government of Jamaica".

Bob was always perfectly at ease in the recording studio. Below: the Wailers in Island's rehearsal studio as they prepare for an appearance on BBC2's *The Old Grey Whistle Test* in 1973.

Alvarita Anderson first met Bob Marley, Peter Tosh and Bunny Livingston when they would walk past the gate of her Aunt Viola's house on Greenwich Park Road as they made their daily trek to Studio One. Rita already had a musical group of her own, the Soulettes, which she had formed with her friend Marlene 'Precious' Gifford and her cousin Constantine 'Dream' Walker. After an audition at Studio One, the Soulettes were passed on to Bob for management and to find material for them. In 1966 Rita married Bob Marley, and worked with him as he developed his Wail'N'Soul'M label. In 1974, she began to work with her husband in a much more public way, as part of the I-Threes, the female backing trio who replaced Peter Tosh and Bunny Livingston: with Judy Mowatt and Marcia Griffiths, Rita Marley came to help define the international sound of Bob's music. Since his death in May 1981, Rita has continued to make music of her own, scoring a reggae hit with 'One Draw', a paean to herb. However, her principal role is as keeper of the faith, not only of her husband's legend, but also of Rastafari.

Growing up in Trench Town, had you heard much about Rastafari?

No. I would see Rastafarian elders and be taught to be scared of them: these people were supposed to be dangerous. They always carried a bag, and you'd be told they'd kill you and put you in that bag. But I'd also feel sympathy for them: 'Oh, poor people - I don't think they are as bad as they say'. You'd see them and they'd say, 'One love', and you'd wonder how people could say that that deal with hate.

Why did they have that reputation?

Society didn't get into the philosophy. They had a name for them - 'Blackheart Man'. They said they were dangerous and they all lived in the gully. And that they were mad from smoking ganja: it mads you. I'd been to high school - even though I was from Trench Town. I was given a little step above the normal living. I was exposed to certain things and saw that these people were innocent. Because of their innocency. But I was still being told to be afraid of Rastafarians - until I met Bob.

Was Bob totally into Rastafari then?

Not really. Not one hundred per cent. A certain awareness of consciousness in terms of black power, which was there all the time. But he didn't know about the philosophy of Rastafari to the fullness.

After we got married I was interested because I was more into a Christian from that time. I was more interested in the spiritual side of things than the worldly side. Then I realised that Rastafari is essentially the same as Christianity, but with maybe a little more freedom. It's more like the Bible says, 'Every man to his own order'.

Rita with Cedella, her eldest daughter born to Bob.

Ziggy: as the eldest son, he was to take on the full weight of his father's legacy.

You used to see Bob and the other Wailers as they walked past your home in Trench Town: were they a very happening group at that time?

They were very popular. It was a hard task to stay in the music and be consistent with hits, because they had 'Simmer Down', 'Put It On', 'Rude Boy' - one hit coming after the other, but they weren't making any money.

What do you think Bob's strength was as a writer?

It was what he had to say in terms of writing what's happening, people's lives, using himself as an example, and being able to identify with street people, the common people.

I heard you were slightly nervous of Bob when you first met him...

His disciplinarian attitude was... You have to be prepared to meet him, and then when you meet him, it's... But behind all of that he was the nicest person, like an angel.

He was very focused...

And firm, about what we were about: if you come to the studio you don't come to joke, you don't come to play. As long as Bob was there that discipline was established.

In 1966, you and Bob moved to Nine Miles, his birthplace in the country. How did you find life there?

I'd never been exposed to country. I'd been in Kingston all my life. It was different: I had to carry water, collect wood to make the fire, and I had to sleep on a little, small bed on the dirt. But it was all out of love.

Because Bob was already exposed to this lifestyle, it was a thrill for him to see me just living it. It was something he had decided he would do eventually - just be a farmer and stay in the country and live. Before he got sick he said he was going to take a break from the music and go and build a house in St Ann's for the children.

Did you write songs with him there?

We did a lot of writing, we did a lot of singing there, sharing a lot of special times, special moments, when I was getting to know the other side of him more so than just being in the studio. We did a lot of songs together. He'd try stuff out on me. "Listen to this one, listen to that one". And look up into the sky and the air - a lot of inspiration coming.

This was the start of the Wail'N'Soul'M label: how did he find that experience?

It was independence for him. Freedom from Coxsone and other record companies. We went back to Trench Town and opened a little record shop: in the daytime it would be a shop and at night time it would be a bedroom - that's where we lived.

Cedella was born and shortly after that you had Ziggy or David as he was christened. Why was he called Ziggy?

I wanted David, because of how he was born at home in Trench Town. It was a home delivery and I'm still into being more spiritual than what the eye sees: and I said, "This little boy must be David". I wasn't even thinking of Bob as being as great as he is today. But I saw Bob as a great writer: sometimes I would call him King David. His appearance is very royal when you look at him, and that was before fame and success and money.

Bob said, "Well, this is Ziggy, Ziggy." And I said, "What is this Ziggy?" and Bob said, "It's football!", a name for - what they call it? - dribbling. They used to call out to Bob, "Ziggy, Bob, ziggy". He was good at that, taking the ball and moving it up and down. That's how Ziggy got that name.

Did Bob talk about the fact that his own father wasn't around?

There was nothing to talk about, really. How can you talk about someone you never know? At one time we tried to get in touch with his brothers; we went as far as going into their office to say that Bob wanted to borrow a tractor to plough down in St Ann's. But their attitude was, "Why you come to us? Yes, Norval might be your father but he didn't have anything here for you". And so we left very disappointed, very upset.

Tell me about the importance of Scratch. What was the chemistry between him and Bob?

Bob always seemed to like to be around people with ideas, people who is thinking something new, people who every time you see them you get an inspiration. So Scratch was that kind of person to Bob. He knew that Bob had something in him different from Bunny and Peter - he always said that.

There is a great vitality to those songs they did together.

It's something about working with people when you can get the kind of communication you need. And that was lacking with the Wailers for a time. With Bunny and Peter... the chemistry after a while started to diminish and Bob felt something was lacking: he knew it, he wasn't able to be as creative as he started out to be. This was where Perry came in as a relief. Because if it was not happening with these two brothers, there was someone else he could get some expression from.

The relationship with Scratch continued for a long time.

Yes. But then Peter and Bunny thought Scratch was a madman. There was a problem there. This was why Bob and Scratch became more of a key than the other two.

Didn't Scratch work with Bob on lots of the Island stuff?

Yes. And when they were in England I think they did some things.

I always heard Scratch worked on Rastaman Vibration?

Not to my knowledge. When *Rastaman Vibration* came in, Bob was really on his own. It was Bob and Fams and Tyrone. We were really bubbling there.

When Burnin' was out, was Bob dispirited with the problems of Bunny and Peter not wanting to tour?

I don't think he would allow anyone to crumble his ambitions.

Like he said in one of his interviews, he could not sit at home and idle; when Ziggy and his children grew up and asked why he didn't go to work to send them to school, what would he have said to them? So he was pushed because he felt he had a responsibility more than the other two guys. And when it started to reach that stage where he was really going after it, Peter and Bunny decided that they weren't going to do the same.

So Bob made the decision to work with you. Do you remember how the subject of the I-Threes first came up?

They were in the studio.

He had problems getting Peter to the studio on time. Little differences were coming up. He said, "I can't work like this. I have to deliver the album to Island Records and we have a tour. Maybe Rita and Marcia and Judy could do something." We were already in our own individual rights doing things. We decided to put the three voices with Bob. I was living at Bull Bay then. Bob sent for me and asked if I could find Marcia and Judy for a song. And it clicked and that was it: we did the whole album instead of one song. And we went on the tour for promotion.

What did you feel about the shooting incident?

The shooting? That evil exists.

When that happened in 1976 it was a confirmation for me that evil does exist. There was no reason to put this plot together. Whoever did it, I don't know. But it still feels like it was politically motivated.

It's too big to be some ordinary gangster thing.

Above: The I-Threes - Rita Marley, Marcia Griffiths and Judy Mowatt - photographed on a rock just offshore from 'Goldeneye', the house where Ian Fleming wrote the James Bond novels.

"I'm a self-taught guitar player. Me like guitarists like Ernest Ranglin." BOB MARLEY

If the 1976 'Smile Jamaica' concert was intended to bring the nation together, no one seemed to have mentioned this to the JLP gunmen who entered the rehearsal area at Bob's house in 56 Hope Road the night before the concert was scheduled. Bob was standing there, peeling an orange; Don Taylor, his manager, had just entered the room when shots rang out, four of which hit Taylor in the area of the lower abdomen. A stray bullet ricocheted across Bob's chest, lodging in his arm. Outside in the car park, Rita Marley was starting up her VW Beetle when shots were fired through the rear window, one of which grazed the side of her head.

profound shift through the catalyst of punk. At first, however, Bob was deeply resistant to what he perceived as simply another manifestation of Babylon. Only later in the year, after Lee 'Scratch' Perry had shown him the positive aspect of this social revolution, did he begin to comprehend the changes taking place, and record the song 'Punky Reggae Party'.

For the meantime, Bob Marley worked away in the studio in the basement of Island Records. As though the shooting had only strengthened his resolve, he was on a creative high, working closely with keyboards player Tyrone Downie who was becoming more prominent as the

Bob and Rita were rushed away: Bob to Strawberry Hill, a beautiful mountain-top retreat owned by Chris Blackwell; Rita to hospital. Armed guards were posted.

The next evening the 'Smile Jamaica' show went ahead as planned. And Bob appeared onstage, his arm in a sling, with Rita, still wearing her hospital night-clothes, as one of his backing singers.

Immediately after the show, Bob left the island on a privately chartered Lear jet. It was to be 15 months before he was to return to Jamaica.

In the first week of 1977 Bob Marley and the Wailers flew to London, taking up residence in a house in Chelsea. The presence of the Tuff Gong added to the collective energy in a city whose artistic thinking was undergoing a

group arranger than Family Man Barrett had been. Songs had flown out of the sessions, many of them inspired by events around the shooting. The new album was to be called *Exodus*, decreed Bob, even though that was one of the only songs he hadn't yet written.

By the end of March all the songs for *Exodus* seemed to have been recorded, but the group worked on in the studio, completing a total of 24 songs. Quickly these were weighed up: the tone of ten of them was perfect for *Exodus*, the first side of which was given over to songs about the shooting. The rest, lighter and more mystical in vein, were put aside for the next album, *Kaya*, which was mixed at Criteria in Miami, a conscious and successful effort to give the record a different feel and sound.

A month after the epochal *Exodus* came out, Bob and the Wailers began a European tour in Paris, 200 miles from the Tuff Gong's temporary home in London, where he had been living in exile since the attempt on his life in Kingston. In a football game in Paris between the Wailers and a group of French journalists, Bob was given a hard tackle; his right foot was badly hurt and the nail torn off the big toe. The toe was already vulnerable: Bob had first injured it in 1975; it had been slashed by another player's pair of rusty running spikes whilst he was playing football on the Boy's Town recreation ground in Trench Town. Although he tried to clean up the wound with cotton and

Bob was determined to get through his tour. Sometimes following a show, as after one of the London dates at the Rainbow Theatre, he would find his boot filled with blood. Those around him noticed that Bob had to keep changing the bandage; clearly the wound was not healing.

In London Bob went to see a Harley Street specialist with Junior Marvin. The doctor told him the toe should be cut off; it had become contaminated and the infection could get into his bloodstream; he also warned him of the danger of cancer. Everyone around Bob began to offer an opinion: he was advised that having his toe removed could ruin his career, and it was suggested that he get a

As his musical stature grew, Bob increasingly confided in his close friends that perhaps he should have been a soccer player instead. Bob's team for this match, in London's Battersea Park, included Neville Garrick, Gillie the juice-man, Bob's spar Trevor Bow and Derek from the Sons Of Jah.

anti-septic, he was never given an anti-tetanus shot. The wound never really healed: Cedella, his daughter, would dress it for him in the evenings. The doctor Bob saw in Paris told him he must stay off his feet, but he didn't heed this advice. The only compromise he made was to wear sandals, which revealed a large bandage on his right foot, and the Tuff Gong performed some shows wearing sandals and the bandage. Even dressed like this, he would still play soccer every day, wincing when the ball banged his foot.

second opinion. Then a doctor in Miami told Bob that a skin-graft would cure the problem, to which he agreed.

Bob Marley's flight touched down at Kingston's Norman Manley airport on 26th February 1978; as it coasted to a halt he was aware that this return to his home country was only viable and valid if it contained a direct effort to end the escalating violent hatred that was tearing Jamaica apart and terrifying its population.

But flying in the face of most predictions, the concert on 22nd April was a resounding success, a focus for the media of the western world. 16 of the island's most significant reggae acts, including Jacob Miller and Inner Circle, the Mighty Diamonds, Trinity, Dennis Brown, Culture, Dillinger, Big Youth, Peter Tosh and Ras Michael

"God never made no difference between black, white, blue, pink or green. People is people, y'know." BOB MARLEY

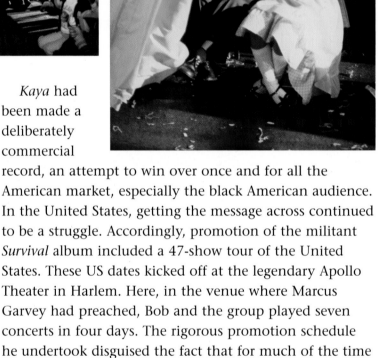

And The Sons Of Negus appeared. To coincide with the event, a new album was released by Bob Marley and the Wailers – *Kaya* was a collection of love songs and, of course, homages to the power of ganja; the album was also to provide a pair of chart singles, 'Satisfy My Soul' and the beautiful 'Is This Love'.

At the show Peter Tosh harangued Michael Manley and Edward Seaga for persecuting ghetto sufferahs for their fondness for herb, and lit up a spliff onstage. Bob, however, seemed in a state of transcendental bliss. Instead of attacking the Prime Minister and leader of the opposition, he attempted to bring them together. During 'Jamming' his dancing delivery and skat extemporising on the lyrics were those of someone taken over by the spirit: "To make everything come true, we've got to be together, yeah, yeah. And to the spirit of the most high, His Imperial Majesty Emperor Haile Selassie I, run lightning, leading the people of the slaves to shake hands... I'm not so good at talking but I hope you understand what I'm trying to say. I'm trying to say, could we have, could we have, up here onstage here the presence of Mr Michael Manley and Mr Edward Seaga. I just want to shake hands and show the people that we're gonna unite... we're gonna unite... we've got to unite..." And he held together the hands of the two opposing politicians. The Peace Concert was the opening salvo of the first world tour: Tuff Gong gone outer-national...

Whilst in Jamaica, Bob spent time with his old spar Scratch Perry. In one day Bob cut four tunes at Black Ark, including 'Black Man Redemption' and 'Rastaman Live Up', both of which came out as singles on Tuff Gong, and were a marked departure from the softer subjects of *Kaya*.

Kaya had been made a deliberately commercial record, an attempt to win over once and for all the American market, especially the black American audience. In the United States, getting the message across continued to be a struggle. Accordingly, promotion of the militant *Survival* album included a 47-show tour of the United States. These US dates kicked off at the legendary Apollo Theater in Harlem. Here, in the venue where Marcus Garvey had preached, Bob and the group played seven concerts in four days. The rigorous promotion schedule he undertook disguised the fact that for much of the time he was operating in a state of sheer exhaustion. By the end of this tour many of those travelling with Bob were extremely worried about his health.

In April 1980, Bob Marley took part in a performance as historic as the Peace Concert and the 'Smile Jamaica' event had been. Except this was in Africa, his spiritual home. On 18th April, the country of Rhodesia was finally being granted independence from rule by the white upstarts who had taken over the country under Prime Minister Ian Smith. And it was changing its name to Zimbabwe. Bob, whose 'Zimbabwe' tune had proved inspirational to the National Liberation Army, was invited to play at the independence celebrations. He performed amidst the ruins of Great Zimbabwe, an enormous pyramid built by Solomon and Sheba. Although blighted by organisational hassles, the show was a colossal success.

Above: At the video shoot for the 1978 single 'Is This Love', at north London's Keskidee Centre, one of the extras in the children's party arranged for the event was a young Naomi Campbell.

The Tuff Gong Uprising tour began in May 1980, starting in Zurich. It continued at a gruelling, breakneck pace. As the bus left 56 Hope Road for Kingston airport at the beginning of the journey to Europe, Mortimer Planner had stood by the gates, bidding farewell and good luck to his brethren. When the vehicle pulled past him, Bob's eyes momentarily caught Planner's. From nowhere a thought ran through the dread elder: "I won't see you again."

The American leg of the tour began in Boston on Sunday 14th September. Then the Wailers touring party drove south to New York City, where they were scheduled to play a pair of shows the following weekend, on September 19th and 20th, at Madison Square Garden, sharing the bill with the Commodores, an effort to broaden Bob's American audience.

At the Essex House on Central Park South champagne and fine wines were being ordered up on room service. Pascaline, a daughter of the Gabonese president who was Bob's latest girlfriend, was ensconced in his suite with him. Limousines would follow the tour bus wherever it went, like some anti-Exodus. New York-based Jamaicans

flooded into the various suites; cocaine freebasing was openly practised; goodtime girls sprawled about the rooms. It was as though everything was disintegrating, everything was falling apart. Bob tucked himself away in his bedroom, often aghast at the bedlam taking place outside his door. As he himself would have described the scene, it was "too much mix-up, mix-up".

The Madison Square Garden shows, however, were a huge success: the performances were tremendous, as was the audience response. "We were ready for that tour," said Family Man. "We and Stevie Wonder were supposed to tour the US. We were going to break reggae big-big in the States, just like in Europe. Then suddenly something came up."

After the first of the two shows on the Saturday night, Bob had seemed inexplicably exhausted. Recovering for the second performance, he left very early from an outing to the Negril night club and returned to the hotel.

The next morning Bob felt nauseous: he needed some fresh air. Attempting to kickstart his life force with some light running, Bob and Alan Cole and a few friends jogged into Central Park, opposite their hotel. Before they had gone far, however, Bob started to collapse, calling out for Cole who caught him before he slumped to the ground. Bob's body seemed to be freezing rigid, and he couldn't move his neck. It hurt him terribly and frightened him. Helped back to the hotel, he recovered after a couple of hours. But the incident had shaken him to his core, and he still felt great pain in his neck region.

Chris Blackwell had long kept an apartment on the top floor of the Essex House. Late on the Monday morning his doorbell rang. It was Bob; even the sense of quiet sadness and physical pain about him could not wither his kingly nature as he told Blackwell the news: that he was suffering from what was apparently an incurable brain tumour and had been given no more than three weeks to live.

This grim news shocked Blackwell. Terrible remorse, even self-recrimination, momentarily took him over. He remembered how Bob had been told by the doctor he saw in 1977 that he should have a check-up every three months. "Everybody kind of forgot about that. But when something like that happens it rushes back. I felt I should have reminded him. I should have insisted he had the check-ups. If only they had, they could have caught it a lot earlier: if he'd had his toe amputated in the first place, it probably would have saved his life."

At the soundcheck at the Stanley Theater in Pittsburgh the next afternoon, there was a break in the routine. Instead of the usual four songs that would be tried out at a soundcheck, Bob only performed a long version of an old

Far left: The moments when Bob Marley brought together Prime Minister Michael Manley and Edward Seaga, the leader of the opposition, at the 1978 Peace Concert. Above: The house at Hope Road where gunmen attacked Bob, Rita and manager Don Taylor. Right: Bob in New York City, September 1980. It was on this visit that he collapsed while running in Central Park (to his left).

Gong International tour of the United States was cancelled. The reason? Bob Marley was suffering from "exhaustion". The group returned to Miami, and then dispersed...

Clearly Bob Marley's legacy has not only lived on, but it has taken a quantum leap. The posthumous *Legend* album, a greatest hits compilation, has sold over 15 million copies, making it one of the biggest selling albums of all time; *Songs Of Freedom*, the Bob Marley box-set released in 1992, sold out its limited edition of one million copies in weeks; a tribute concert in Jamaica's Oracabessa at the end of 1999 drew the cream of current black artists - as well as many white ones - to interpret his masterful music.

Beyond sales figures, however, time has given Bob Marley a larger stature. Now he is seen as a hero figure, in the classic mythological sense. To westerners his apocalyptic truths prove inspirational and life-changing; in the Third World his impact is similar, except that it goes further. Not just amongst Jamaicans, but also amongst the Hopi Indians of New Mexico and the Maoris of New Zealand, in Indonesia, in India, even - especially - in those parts of West Africa from which slaves were plucked and taken to the New World, Bob Marley is seen as the Redeemer figure returning to lead this planet out of confusion. Some will come out and say it directly: that Bob Marley is the reincarnation of Jesus Christ long awaited by much of the world. In such an interpretation of his life, the cancer that killed Bob Marley is inevitably described as a modern version of a crucifixion.

Even confronted by a future of such grim uncertainty, Bob managed to never lose his wry view of life. Two weeks after his collapse, his death was being reported in the US media; he put out a statement in which his characteristic dry sense of humour was clearly still in evidence: "They say that living in Manhattan is hell, but..."

Wailers tune, 'Keep On Moving', sitting for much of the time on the drum-riser beside Carly. Although it involved only one tune, it was the longest soundcheck any of the group remembered. Most of them felt very sad indeed.

That night's show was extraordinary: Bob came onstage unannounced and the group played a 90-minute version of their show that exploded into a succession of encores: 'Redemption Song', 'Coming In From The Cold', 'Could You Be Loved', 'Is This Love', and 'Work'. This was literally what he was doing. 'Work' was the last song Bob Marley ever performed onstage, as he gave his absolute best. "That show had to be great," said Junior Marvin. "Everyone was aware that Bob wasn't at all well and that it could be the last show. We were just hoping that it wouldn't be." Later that night, at Rita's instigation, a press release was put out. Bob Marley and the Wailers' Tuff

HON. ROBERT NE

Bob Marley's funeral service was held in Kingston's National Heroes Arena. He had been given radiation treatment to fight the cancer invading his body, and as a result his dreadlocks had fallen out. Rita, his wife, had kept the locks and they were woven into a wig which was placed on his head. Sharing Bob's coffin with him were his worn copy of the Bible and his Gibson guitar.

After various efforts to cure him - by both conventional and alternative medicine, in the United States and Germany - it became apparent to the Tuff Gong that it was time to go home to Jamaica.

He made it no further than Miami, where he arrived in the early hours of 10th May 1981: his condition was judged sufficiently serious for him to be immediately checked into the city's Cedars of Lebanon hospital.

That afternoon his children Cedella and Ziggy visited him in his private room. They found their father surrounded by a group of evangelists who had flown up from Jamaica to be with him. Confident that their father was in safe hands, the children left the hospital and returned to the Miami house of their grandmother, Mrs Cedella Booker, Bob's mother.

MARLEY O.M.

HON. ROBERT NESTA MARLEY O.M.

"If God had nuh given me a song to sing, I wouldn't have a song to sing. The song comes from God, all the time." BOB MARLEY

Shortly after 11.30 a.m. the next morning, Cedella heard the telephone ring. Picking it up at the same time as her uncle Gibson, she heard the voice of Diane Jobson, a close friend of the family, telling her uncle that Bob Marley had passed on to the next life.

As she held the receiver to her ear, her attention was caught by a movement across the room: on the mantelpiece she saw a framed photograph of her father shift slightly. Cedella looked across at it, and Bob's eyes gazed deeply into her own.

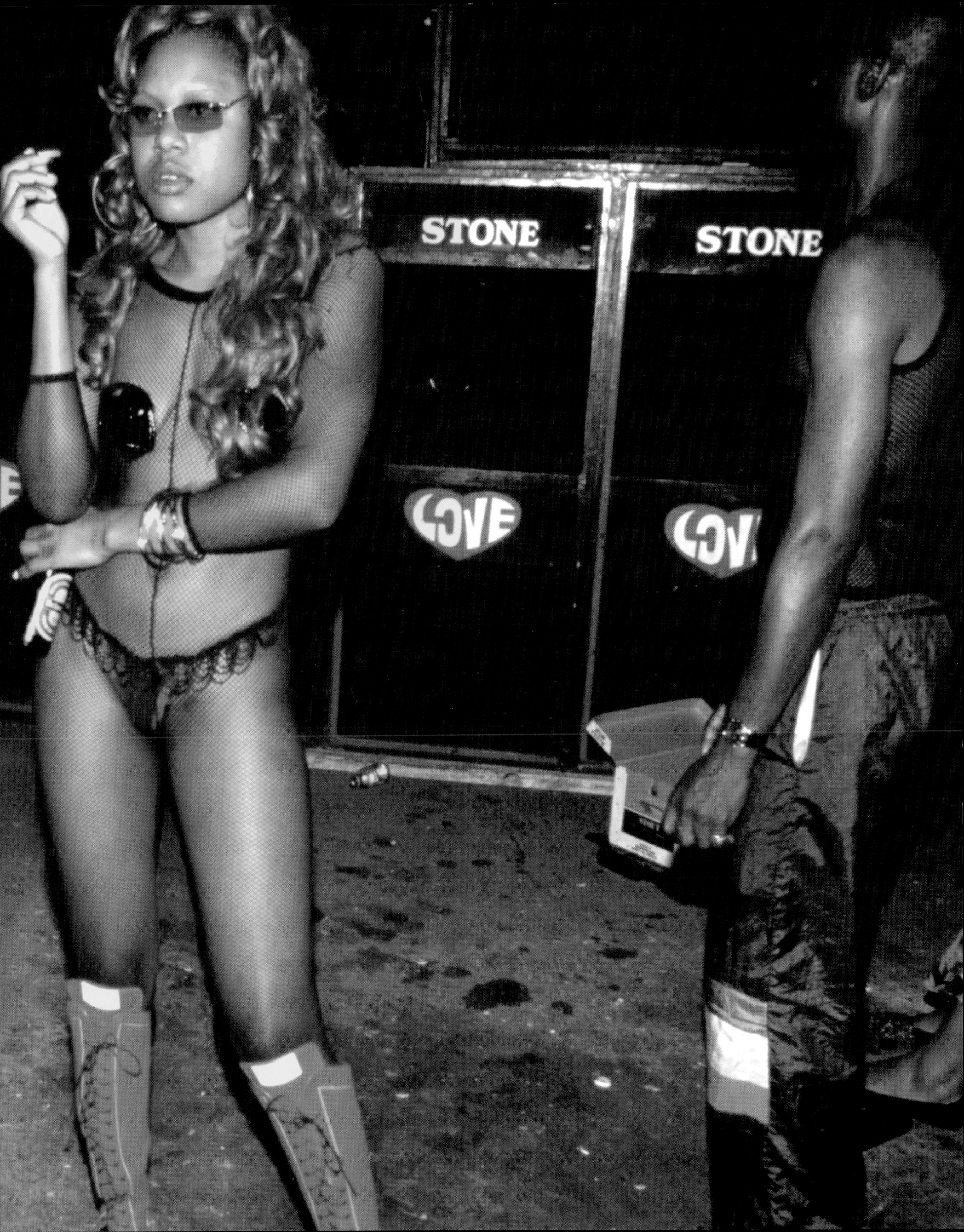
STONE
STONE
LOVE

Dancehall, the marriage of digital beats and slackness: that moment and music in which lyrics about guns, women's body parts and men's sexual prowess come together, epitomised by 'Wicked In Bed', Shabba Ranks' international hit. This rough and very upfront style of

DANCE

street reggae music, a form which literally originated in the dancehall, was first developed in the late 1970s as Henry 'Junjo' Lawes set off a flood of productions. As digital technology took over in the mid-1980s, dancehall adapted naturally, resulting in ragga - short for the self-explanatory 'raggamuffin'.

Around 1993 a spiritual moment in ragga was underway, one that climaxed with Buju Banton's epic *Til Shiloh* set in 1995. In the 1990s ancient African forms of rhythm were being reproduced digitally. But is this music so simply separated in conscious styles versus slackness?

HALL

No; it is forever more complex than that. Jamaican popular music has invariably incorporated both the slack and the spiritual, because both lie at the heart of African popular music. A figure like Lady Saw captures this duality: on the one hand reviled for her performances and lyrics, she also has a side that is extremely roots'n'culture and conscious. Her main stick is that people should be more concerned by the slack way in which society is run.

At the beginning of the 1980s Jamaica, along with other Caribbean islands, became a trans-shipment point for the cocaine trade. The potential to acquire fabulous wealth was shadowed by the possibility - sometimes by the probability - of violent death. After Edward Seaga's Jamaica Labour Party had decisively won the 1980 election for the right, a mood reflected throughout much of the world, political gunmen became freelance operators: many moved to the United States where the Jamaican posses controlled the street-level distribution and marketing of the decade's new superdrug, crack cocaine.

On the island itself, vicious turf wars took place as dons fought for control of the distribution of a drug that in Jamaica was priced for even the poorest sufferah's pocket. Many a ghetto youth lost his life in the hails of bullets and cutlass slashes that seemed to go hand-in- hand with the drug.

At the close of the 1990s the ends of such crucial local superstars as Dennis Brown and I-Roy were hastened by their involvement with crack. And the death by shooting of Henry 'Junjo' Lawes in London in 1999 was widely believed to have been connected to his involvement with drug posses.

Yet for several years Junjo Lawes had been the most influential and important figure in the development of dancehall music. In the early 1980s he was the hottest reggae producer around, the originator of the 'dancehall' style that has dominated Jamaican music since the death of Bob Marley in 1981.

Such names as Yellowman, Eek-A-Mouse, Barrington Levy, and Josey Wales all owed their careers to Lawes. More established acts like John Holt, the Wailing Souls, Alton Ellis and Ken Boothe also enjoyed revivals after recording over Lawes' rhythm tracks for his Volcano label, released in the UK by Greensleeves Records. The first album to be released in the UK was Barrington Levy's *Englishman*, which was followed by no fewer than 42 others.

They included Eek-A-Mouse's record *Wa-Do-Dem*, Yellowman's *Mr Yellowman* and *Zungguzungguguzungguzeng*, the classic series of Scientist Dub albums, the Wailing Souls' superb *Firehouse Rock*, and albums by artists as

Above: Pictured with some brethren during the run-up to the 1980 Jamaican election, Henry 'Junjo' Lawes was one of the most significant producers of the island's music; he has firmly branded his mark on the entire development of 'dancehall' music.

diverse as Hugh Mundell, John Holt, General Echo, Michigan and Smiley, Don Carlos and Josey Wales. Few artists recording in the dancehall era did not record for Junjo. He even reached the British charts with his pairing of the deejays Clint Eastwood and General Saint.

Lawes' murder in a drive-by shooting in Harlesden, north-west London, reflected the uneasy relationship between music, crime and politics that has long characterised the reggae business. It was like a metaphor for dancehall, the rough, immensely catchy 'street' style of reggae.

Lawes' ghetto credentials were impeccable: born in 1960 in Olympic Way in the slums of West Kingston, he spent much of his youth in McKoy Lane in nearby Whitfield Town - "badman territory", as one person who knew him described it - where he was a teenager during the lethal undeclared civil war of the 1970s. The neighbourhood was the fiefdom of Jack Massop, the father of Claudie Massop, a 'ranking' gunman for Prime Minister Michael Manley's People's National Party (PNP) and an acquaintance of Bob Marley. But although he moved with the PNP badmen, Lawes was never a gunman himself.

Due to the efforts of the legendary record producer Bunny 'Striker' Lee, who was always keen to discourage local youth from such a potentially lethal existence, Lawes veered away from following a similar career and in 1978 began singing with the Grooving Locks trio. The same year, at the tender age of 18, he began to produce records, working first with Linval Thompson.

Within twelve months Lawes had booked a series of sessions at Channel One studio, employing the Roots Radics group as backing band: the sessions were to alter the sound of Jamaican music. The tough sound of the Radics, who often employed old Studio One rhythms, was slower and more penetrating than the 'rockers' style of the Revolutionaries, Kingston's other dominant studio house-band; thanks to his street-corner connections, Lawes was assiduously adept at sizing and signing up the newest talent and for these studio dates he used the mixing desk skills of Hopeton Brown, a young engineer who became

For Adults Only

POT
ON

WELCOME
TO
_SON'S JOINT

I.T.S. Co-op

STRONG TO
FIGHT ANY MAN
THAT IS WELL
FED & FIT
IN THE BLUE
ROOM

RANKING SLACKNESS

Playing the part of benevolent despot that is the stance of every ghetto youth striving for what in Jamaica is known as 'donship', Lawes was known for the uncharacteristic financial respect with which he would treat his artists. "I no really check fe money," he said. "Every man gwan 'ave a equal share, an artist, a producer, instrument player and everybody. The set-up now is unlevelled."

"I always found him to be a straightforward person to deal with," said Chris Sedgwick of Greensleeves Records. "Right from the start, he made arrangements for us to pay many of the artists' royalties direct to them. He struck us as pretty fair."

Joining the Jamaican exodus to New York in the mid-1980s, Lawes attempted to set up Volcano there. He had friends, however, who were on the fringes of the drug posses and Lawes was sentenced to a prison term in the United States, and deported back to Jamaica in 1991.

On his return he worked with several artists, including Cocoa Tea, Ninjaman, and John Holt once again. But it proved hard to emulate his rapid success of the previous decade.

famous under the sobriquet of 'Scientist' (eventually releasing such records under that name for Lawes as *Heavyweight Dub Champion*). As a result, Barrington Levy's *Bounty Hunter* album, which emerged from these Channel One sessions, came to be considered a classic.

Success came fast. Soon Lawes was producing archetypal hits like Michigan and Smiley's 'Diseases', Frankie Paul's 'Pass The Tushenpeng', and John Holt's 'Police In Helicopter'. The astonishingly prodigious Yellowman, who released sixteen albums between 1982 and 1983, recorded several of them for Lawes.

To combat the indifference of Jamaican radio programmers, Lawes launched his Volcano sound system in 1983. Using his own unlimited supply of dub plates, Volcano became Jamaica's top sound system, playing almost nightly all over the island.

For the two or three years following the death of Bob Marley, Lawes came up with the best rhythms emerging from Jamaica, dancehall-based street music that was much rougher and rawer than the image of reggae the Tuff Gong had presented.

When he was shot on 14th June 1999, Junjo Lawes had been in London since the previous Christmas. He was planning to return to Jamaica the following week. "He is so much a product of Jamaica - the Jamaican badman-producer for whom it all goes wrong," said Steve Barrow. "Junjo was a man who things happened around, a ghetto version of Duke Reid."

Even Lawes' end is an archetypal dancehall story. He was by no means the only dominant figure in the music, however. Although he directed the beginnings of the style, he had left Jamaica by the time it had taken the leap forward into what was known as 'ragga': music played almost entirely on digital machines. True, the very style of the Roots Radics had pushed the music in that direction, as had Sly and Robbie's self-explanatory 'robotic' sound on tunes like Sugar Minott's 'Rub A Dub Sound' - a tribute to the rising power of the syndrum, a sound with which drummer Sly Dunbar was especially taken. But the Blood Fire Posse, led by Paul Blake, had also made a pair of records whose semi-computerised sound was revolutionary in 1983 and '84 when they were released: 'Rub A Dub Soldier' (in which, employing the bassline from Slim Smith's classic Studio One hit 'Never Let Go', Blake proclaimed he was fighting to keep the rockers alive) and 'Every Posse Get Flat'. The first record in particular seemed to be moving the entirety of Jamaican music in a new direction.

The king of digital dancehall, however, was a man who had adopted for himself a regal title, as though he wished there to be no doubt of his position: Lloyd 'King Jammy' James, who had promoted himself from being Prince Jammy. Starting out in his native Waterhouse district of Kingston as a builder of sound system equipment, Jammy graduated to working as an engineer with King Tubby during the late 1970s. Existing at the same kind of street level as Junjo Lawes, he came across many up-and-coming artists, like Junior Reid, Echo Minott, and Half Pint, and

Opposite top left: Barrington Levy was 15 when his first tunes were released as part of the initial flurry of sessions by Junjo Lawes at Channel One.
Opposite below: Following their 'Rub A Dub Style' hit, Papa Michigan and General Smiley set the tone for the newly developing dancehall music with their 1979 smash 'Nice Up The Dance', one of countless records that had the Soul Vendors' 'Real Rock' as its rhythmic base. Working with Junjo Lawes, the deejay double-act had a further huge tune with 'Diseases', a warning of the consequences of sexual profligacy, set to the rhythm of Alton Ellis's 'Mad Mad'.
Right: His 'singjay' style set Eek-A-Mouse well ahead of the pack when his masterly 'Wa -Do-Dem' tune showed that here was an up-and-coming vocalist who had paid attention to contemporary sound system deejays. Born Ripton Hilton, the name under which he first recorded, his new professional moniker came from a racehorse he had ill-advisedly backed.

recorded the debut album by Black Uhuru, who hailed from that area. His Super Power sound system turned up a number of deejays, including Admiral Bailey, Chaka Demus, Major Worries, and Lieutenant Stitchie.

Among the vocalists who were to come to the fore with Jammy were Nitty Gritty, King Kong and Tenor Saw. It said much about the culture of dancehall that both Nitty Gritty and Tenor Saw were shot to death, and both in the USA - Nitty Gritty in New York in 1991 and Tenor Saw found dead by a Texas roadside in 1988, a 'drogs bisness' killing.

ring the alarm/Another sound is dying," he describes the end of a sound system.

By the time Tenor Saw passed on, King Jammy had undoubtedly become the number one figure in digital dancehall. Like most of the best cultural innovations, this had happened largely by chance. In 1985 Jammy recorded Wayne Smith on a tune called 'Under Me Sleng Teng'. The record became a phenomenon. Allegedly, Smith and Noel Bailey, another young singer, discovered one of the rock rhythms on a Casio Music Box - a rhythm

Tenor Saw's legacy is particularly exceptional: his 'Lots Of Sign' tune on Sugar Minott's Youth Promotion label always stands out, for example; and he was the first artist to be recorded on dubplate for Minott's Youth Promotion sound system by Jah Stitch, the selecter. However, it was the 1985 tune 'Ring The Alarm', a magnificent record, for which he became legendary.

Its rhythm was an overdubbed cut of 'Stalag 17', the 1973 organ instrumental by Ansel Collins, but the lyrics and Tenor Saw's delivery were what made it: *"Hey, woah,*

which carries a distinct resemblance to that of Eddie Cochran's 'Something Else'. Slowing it down, they turned it into the reggae rhythm behind the tune; another version of this story is less prosaic: Smith simply found it on his computerised keyboard.

Like an equivalent of English garden-shed punk rock, the tune opened the way to an array of young artists and independent producers, and reggae has never looked back: it set the way for singers straight off the street to record simply, without studio musicians.

Eventually there were over 400 versions of the 'Sleng Teng' rhythm available. Jamaican music always had continually cannibalised itself in order to move ahead, and in the middle of the 1980s reggae became 'ragga,' short for raggamuffin.

King Jammy was at the very top of this development, both with his productions on his Jammys label (spelt, appropriately enough, Jammy$) and his sound system.

The redoubtable Young Turk team of bassist Wycliffe 'Steely' Johnson and drummer Cleveland 'Clevie' Browne, Steely and Clevie, provided the rhythms, like a junior version of Sly and Robbie. Meanwhile, the beautiful style of sax-player Dean Fraser - one of the few live studio musicians to outlast this computerised change - would be interwoven into tracks created by computers. Sanchez and Thriller U, two of the most popular singers of the digital world, recorded extensively for King Jammy.

Above: Tenor Saw's epochal 'Ring The Alarm', which was released in 1985, remains a dancehall staple even today. Tenor Saw had learnt the ropes with Sugar Minott's very influential Youth Promotion sound system, based in West Kingston, the selecter being the excellent deejay Jah Stitch; Barry Brown, Junior Reid, Trevor Hartley, Ranking Joe and Ranking Dread were further graduates of Minott's youth training scheme.
Overleaf: In 1980 Johnny Osbourne released his *Truth And Rights* LP for Studio One. A masterly, understated set, it is a classic album. One of the most popular singers in Jamaica at the time, he had a huge success in 1983 with 'Water Pumping', and the hits continued throughout the decade. A major artist.

As *The Virgin Encyclopedia Of Reggae* says of King Jammy, "It is impossible to overstate his contribution to Jamaican music, because, as the top producer throughout the digital era, he has altered the sound of reggae music without ever losing touch with its foundation - the sound system."

Often using the songwriting skills of Mikey Bennett, Jammy had over 150 albums on his back catalogue by the end of the 1980s - by which time Robert 'Bobby Digital' Dixon, who had joined Jammy as his extremely able second-in-command, had set up on his own as a rival.

Bobby Digital arrived at Jammy's in 1985, at a time when Steely and Clevie's computerised rhythm tracks were coming to the fore. As Jammy's number two, Digital helped develop such artists as Cocoa Tea (considered by some as "the Bob Marley of the 1980s"), Chaka Demus, Sanchez, Admiral Bailey, Shabba Ranks and Pinchers. In 1988, however, Bobby Digital quit Jammy's, setting up his own studio and Digital B label, as well as the Heatwave sound system. For Shabba his hits included the classics 'Wicked Inna Bed' and 'Gal Yuh Good'. He also worked with Ninjaman, and discovered such new talent as Cobra and Tony Rebel.

During the early 1990s Digital was prominent in pushing such ghetto artists as Terror Fabulous, Jigsy King, and Roundhead - in 1992 he recorded Garnett Silk's debut album, which resulted in a US contract with Atlantic Records.

The first pretender to challenge Jammy, however, had been Hugh 'Redman' James. Another former soundman, James for a time became a prolific producer, with a spurt of hits from 1987 until the end of the decade, most notably with Conroy Smith's 'Dangerous'. Employing the ubiquitous Steely and Clevie, Redman

also worked with Carl Meeks, Courtney Melody, Thriller U and Clement Irie, the evergreen John Holt, and the omnipresent major talent who is Frankie Paul.

Another contender for Jammy's crown was Winston Riley, a former member of the Techniques, who worked with Super Cat, Red Dragon, Flourgon, and Admiral Tibet, among others. King Tubby also emerged as a rival. Tubby launched his Firehouse, Waterhouse and Taurus labels when he opened his new studio in 1985.

Left: A sweet-voice singer associated with the first burst of raw dancehall records of the early 1980s, Calvin 'Cocoa Tea' Scott had emerged from the same sound system circuits as the new breed of deejays. Working with Jammy, Gussie Clarke and Junjo Lawes among others, he was a devout dreadlocked Rasta. Above: Jamaica's number one saxophonist, Dean Fraser is a familiar feature of the classiest records emerging from the island. As a member of the We The People Band in the 1970s, he backed Dennis Brown and appeared on countless sides by Joe Gibbs, for whom he recorded his first LP, *Black Horn Man*. His star rose far higher, however, after an extraordinarily heartfelt performance of Bob Marley's 'Redemption Song' at the 1981 Sunsplash, the year of Bob's death. Fraser works regularly with producers like Carlton Hines and Phillip 'Fattis' Burrell. Right: Working with Sky and Robbie, Ini Kamoze first hit the charts with 'Trouble You A Trouble Me'. In late 1994 he found himself at the top of the US charts with his excellent tune 'Hot Stepper'; the *Lyrical Gangsta* album that followed was targeted very much at the US hiphop audience who had bought that hit.

NINJAMAN

ANTHONY B

JUNIOR REID

JUNIOR DELGADO

PATRA

MR VEGAS

LONE RANGER

GENERAL DEGREE

SUGAR MINOTT

SHAGGY

RED RAT

BUCCANEER

EVERTON BLENDER

"A lot of people talking today about dancehall music. But dancehall music was from before I was born."

DENNIS ALCAPONE

Dancehall's diversity is its strength: from patriarchs like Sugar Minott through international crossover stars like Shaggy to cutting edge deejays like Mr Vegas, it cuts a broad swathe through contemporary music of all genres. Meanwhile, Rastafarian vocalists like Freddie McGregor (below, in traditional attire) continue to draw crowds both young and old. McGregor is now established as one of the elder statesmen of reggae.

Tubby largely took a backseat on the productions - Noel 'Phantom' Gray became his principal engineer following the departure of Professor. Sugar Minott's 'Hard Time Rock' was his first hit, but Anthony Red Rose gave him an icon-like dancehall smash with 'Tempo' (a misspelling of Temper), a number one tune. Tubby, one of the major innovative musical figures of the 20th century, was murdered on 6th February 1989.

Donovan Germain, who had begun producing records in New York in the 1970s, set up Penthouse in Kingston in 1987 at 56 Slipe Road, close by Augustus 'Gussie' Clarke's Music Works studio. Stretching into the 1990s, Germain was to bring to the fore such talented new acts as Buju Banton, General Degree, Cobra, Tony Rebel and Cutty Ranks, a serious rival to Shabba Ranks.

Despite the reputation of Shabba (born Rexton Gordon in 1965 in St Ann's) for 'slackness', many of his records – 'Hard And Stiff', 'Love Punaany Bad', and 'Ca'an Dun', for example - were actually ironic 'reality' tunes. Unfortunately, Shabba metaphorically shot himself in the foot when he appeared on the British television show *The Word*, attempting to defend the homophobia expressed in Buju Banton's 1992 'Boom Bye Bye' tune. After his remarks had been picked up by the media around the world, his career never really recovered. A remarkable performer, Shabba Ranks remains a great artist. (Anyway, forget the controversy: in the world of early 1990s dancehall, status and prestige was all, and Shabba owned a Mercedes with gold-plated bumper bars, the zenith of most deejays' dreams.)

By the middle of the 1990s, however, several more artists had emerged onto a similarly stellar level. Of these, Rodney 'Bounty Killer' Pryce was the most militant and powerful.

Influenced most of all by Brigadier Jerry and Ranking Joe, Bounty Killer (or Bounti Killa - there is little standardised spelling in Jamaica) was encouraged by his cousin, the deejay John Wayne, to voice his debut 'Gun

Must Done', appearing at first as Bounty Hunter. Recording under the auspices of King Jammy and his family, Bounty released numerous hits. In 1995 he stepped away from the Jammy's fold, forming his own Pryceless Records, immediately recording a double album, *My Experience*: the record sold very strongly indeed, as much outside of Jamaica, where it was a big hit with many hiphop fans.

Beenie Man, his closest contemporary rival for hottest Jamaican deejay, wore his soul on his red, gold and green sleeve; despite superb paeans to downtown life like the anthemic 'Slam', tunes like his powerful reality song 'Freedom and Blessed' (*"Yuh los'/Yuh better walk on the right path"*), the title track of his invigorating 1995 LP, a tribute to Haile Selassie, were dedicated as much to the creator - as are many tunes on the *Blessed* album.

Left: Lawd have mercy... More than any other deejay, it is Rodney 'Bounty Killer' Pryce who speaks for the youth of the Jamaican ghetto. Brought up in Trench Town, Seaview Gardens and Riverton City, he began to deejay at the age of twelve, developing the various vocal styles and mannerisms that have become integral to this most artistic of ragga deejays.

Above: The dreadlocked Capleton, a raucous dancehall DJ whose early tunes in 1990 and 1991 like 'Bumbo Red' and 'Rough Rider' were as antediluvian with regard to women as Buju Banton's views of gays, had a conversion to consciousness that was almost as Biblical as that later experienced by Buju. He announced he was taking up Rastafari, and worked with the African Star sound system, which specialises in contemporary dancehall rhythms with conscious lyrics. Capleton later became part of Philip 'Fattis' Burrell's Exterminator posse and appeared to have found an artistic soulmate in Sizzla.

Shabba Ranks

was the first dancehall artist to break out of Jamaica in an international style. Although he recorded 'Heat Under Sufferers Feet' in 1985, his first hit did not come until he recorded 'Needle Eye Punany' - hence an understandable reputation for slackness - for Wittys in New York in 1988. The massive seller 'Wicked In Bed', released the following year, pushed Shabba on his way to becoming a crossover star, the world's best-known raggamuffin.

Born in 1969 in Galina, St Mary, Marion 'Lady Saw' Hall took her stage-name from her idol, Tenor Saw. After working with local sound systems, she quickly developed a reputation as an X-rated deejay: her first hit was the fetchingly named 'Stab Up The Meat', and a later tune was titled 'Peanut Punch Mek Man Shit Up Gal Bed'. But Saw could also perform conscious tunes, such as 'Glory Be To God' and 'Ask God For A Miracle', as well as more mellow country tunes like 'Give Me a Reason'. A fantastically witty live performer, Lady Saw deserves full international success.

When did you start deejaying?

I start deejaying in 1990. I started in the dancehall when I was 15 years old. But in 1990 was the time when I get busted and get big like this. Get bust out of the dancehall. And it's been good ever since.

Why did things start happening then?

I was first working at the Free Zone. But the job wasn't cut out for me, so then I leave. I told the girls I would start going to the studio. And I started going to the studio in '91. Back then there wasn't any recording studio in Galina, St Mary, so I had to come to Kingston. So it took a while.

As a woman coming from the country with no track record, was this difficult?

It wasn't difficult. Not once. During my career what I have got is a lot of criticism. People criticise me and say, "She is so lewd, so raw". But I always have fans out there who will really stand by my side, and say, "Lady Saw is the best, and we love her anyway".

The first records I made were good, but nobody paid any attention to me. I saw guys doing X-rated stuff and getting away with it. So I thought I'd try doing it too. And it worked. I have no regrets. My first X-rated song was 'If The Man Lef'. It went well - that was the one that got me right here today. And then 'Stab Up The Meat'. The lyrics are very bad, very raw, real X-rated.

How do you feel about doing X-rated lyrics?

Sometimes after doing them, I think, "Oh my Gawd: I was bad tonight". But then it's part of the job: if I go onstage and nobody really responds to me, it give me a bad vibe.

Do you become a different person on stage?

Uh-uh. I become a different person because when it's time to work... I'm shy here sitting down with you - sometimes people see that in me. But when I go onstage people always ask me if I turn a button or something, because I go way out: I say anything. I do whatever I want to do. But offstage I'm Marion, not Lady Saw: cool and down-to-earth.

When I come onstage I know I have to bust the place up. So I just go up there and do whatever. It's not something that I plan: I just go up onstage and whatever happen in the mind, I just do it. Sometimes I get the crowd to mingle with me, and tease them a little. It's very productive: it feels good.

One of the things about your performances is that they are very funny...

My performances are very funny: people say Lady Saw is not just an entertainer or performer: she's also an actress - I can make people laugh and feel good going home. And that gives me a great feeling too.

Do you get criticised in the media in Jamaica?

I have been criticised a lot over the years. But it's less recently. I think I'm too tough for them, so they have to just love me and let me go through. I'm too tough.

What about your style, Lady Saw? Which deejays were you into?

I used to listen to Tenor Saw - that's where I took my name from. All the females - a lot. But ever since I became popular I listen to Buju Banton, Luciano, Beenie Man, Bounty Killer. I think they are four tough artists.

Certainly Luciano is part of the new conscious movement: do you think what you do is conscious as well?

What I do is 'reality', really. Sex is reality, because we all have sex. But Luciano is a different person: knowing him, he's also a sweet person. No matter how raw Lady Saw is, Luciano always excludes that when we meet in person: he speaks to me just as Marion. He doesn't care about what I do onstage: it is the person who is deep within you that he cares about. So I admire him a lot.

And the conscious movement: what do you think of that?

It is good. They're going back to the roots. I do sometimes. Back to Bob Marley, Jimmy Cliff, and all the conscious men. Back to roots reggae: everybody can't just chose one way. Sometimes I go back to that too, because I did 'Oh Lord, Please Work A Miracle'.

What do you think to Bob Marley?

He is great. Brilliant. The best really. Because right now people are talking about Bob Marley as though he is still alive. His songs still live on, and give you a deep feeling.

Do you think the position of women in Jamaica has changed in recent years?

There's been a lot of females, really,
but sometimes producers say, "Women don't sell". Lady Saw will sell, Tanya Stevens is doing good, but they don't really go out and voice a lot of females. Rita Marley, Judy Mowatt and Marcia Griffiths - they've been holding the pace for a long while, ever since I was a child. But we need more women. So whenever I am onstage I look out and see females. I call them up onstage so they can do their thing and then a producer can recognise them. We're working on it.

What do you think to women like Nanny, the great Maroon leader?

Nanny was a very strong woman.
I used to read about her when I was going to primary school and how tough she was in the struggle for her people. I think we need more tough women like her, and everything will work out better. Because sometimes we are

too shy and too timid to say what we want and to stand up for what we believe in. So I think we should do more of that. And she still lives on.

Who are your favourite artists in Jamaica right now? And how do you judge them?

As I said, my favourite artists are Beenie Man, Bounty Killer, Buju Banton and Luciano. Luciano is a cultural deejay, very conscious, and a great performer. He can perform for hours and not get tired. Beenie Man is another great performer - he'll perform for hours too, and still move a crowd. Bounty Killer is very talented when he comes to writing songs. Bounty Killer can take an old song and make it into a new one and it becomes a big hit. He is very good with lyrics.

Buju Banton always stands up for what he believes in - I was watching him recently in an interview... He always says what he feels and doesn't let people go behind his back.

Why have you started to manage yourself?

I started managing myself because I can trust me, and I believe in myself. If I'm getting $8000 for a show, if someone starts booking it for me I end up with $6000 or less. I can go out there and talk for myself.

You don't have any children, Lady Saw: that's quite unusual for a woman of your age in Jamaica.

Maybe God is protecting me, or I'm protecting myself. I think most Jamaican girls have kids so early because times are very hard and they depend on a man to give them money on a Friday so they can look good and go to the dancehall. They don't protect themselves sexually, so they get caught up. Kids are having kids.

Like Bounty, a man of the ghetto, Beenie was a consummate professional: although only 21 when *Blessed* was released, Beenie Man already had been performing for fifteen years - at the age of six he was already guesting on records as Boy Wonder. In his mid-teens he could be seen at sound system events like the celebrated House of Leo, dancing on his own, a one-man posse - though at that stage Beenie Man had less recognition than he had had almost a decade earlier.

Beenie Man's infectious music constantly bubbled under in the United States. At the 1996 Gavin Black Music Convention in Atlanta, he was called up onstage during the performance by the Fugees to add his deejay prowess to their mix. The crowd went nuts.

"Some youth nuh really understand the concept of Rasta," said Beenie Man. "They just a sell Rasta, put on some locks and jump up and down saying 'Selassie I'. I'm not into all that: it no really mek sense. Yuh have to

"Mi nuh jump 'pon no bandwagon t'ing," insisted Beenie Man. "Yuh just have to deal with life like yuh suppose to, see?"

be creative, love original stuff at all times."Along with producer Patrick Roberts, Beenie Man helped establish the Shocking Vibes label, which featured, among others, fellow deejays Snagga Puss, Silver Cat (with whom Beenie duetted on the huge hit 'Chronic'), and the highly rated Frisco Kid.

Whereas once upon a time reggae had been considered by non-Caribbeans as a kind of joke music, it emerged as a specific global force during the early 1990s. As well as the

There was no doubt about it: the youthful music of dancehall was immensely commercial. Although Sony tried to push the lascivious Patra, major record labels missed out on the woman who could have taken a slice of the Madonna market if promoted in the right way - Lady Saw. Internationally, the most extraordinary turnaround occurred with Buju Banton, whose move from dancehall deejay to wise conscious artist was a conversion of appropriately Biblical proportions.

reggae riffs and samples that were omnipresent in rock and especially dance music like Jungle, Jamaican music experienced a host of international break-outs. 1995 saw the colossal global success of Diana King, whose blend of R'n'B and reggae styling made her 'Shy Guy' song, strongly featured in the hit movie *Bad Boys*, perhaps the most perfect pop record of that year. Shaggy, Inner Circle, and particularly Chaka Demus and Pliers all sold records on a huge scale worldwide, giving the lie to the silence of the music on a international scale during the 1980s - a stunned response, one always felt, to the death of Bob Marley in May 1981.

Inspired by his uncle, who played drums for Jimmy Cliff, dancehall superstar Beenie Man began deejaying at the age of five. Working with King Jammy's, Volcano and other sound systems, Beenie Man achieved considerable popularity, capitalised on by Bunny Lee who recorded him for an album, *The Ten Year Old DJ Wonder*. During his teens, Beenie disappeared from the music scene, but returned in the 1990s with 'Wicked Man', the first of a series of unending smash hits. His relationship with Carlene the Dancehall Queen only enhanced the handsome star's glamour quotient. Becoming part of the Shocking Vibes team, his status rose even higher, and he was one of the stars of the film *Dancehall Queen*. His *Blessed* album included 'Slam', the dancehall tune of 1995, but his *Maestro* and *Many Moods of Moses* sets were equally excellent. In 1998, Beenie Man reached the UK Top Ten with 'Who Am I'.

Emerging in 1991 like a punk rock iconoclast of dancehall, Buju Banton hit with a string of controversial tunes - 'Love Mi Browning' (a testament to his fondness for light-skinned girls), 'Batty Rider', 'Bogle Dance' and 'Big It Up'. After the controversial release of the violently homophobic 'Boom Bye Bye', however, it seemed Buju - born Mark Myrie in Kingston in 1973 - had gone too far. Yet he more than redeemed himself with 1995's *Til Shiloh*, a work of profound maturity.

When you released Til Shiloh, *many people were surprised that you had gone conscious.*

I and I make music according to how I feel. The music I put out is the music that

bust into my soul. When the masses hear the music, what come into their mind I don't know. But what I want them to understand is the fullness of what this particular music is dealing with. It's not about the vessel, but what is in the vessel.

Where do you get the inspiration for your songs?

Inspiration for songs is a everyday thing from what happen around me. Things you see

in society, things that happen around the world - things that you see that no one else seems to see. These are inspiration enough to make even a blind man see and a dumb man speak.

What drew you to use Nyabinghi drumming?

The Nyabinghi form of drumming has been here since creation. Originated in Uganda, eastern Africa, by

the Queen and her followers and her crew. Then it was brought to Jamaica and Rastaman embraced it. It is a firm order and the beginning of many things in the drum: and the drum is the very first instrument in creation. So all musicians have to learn the drum and succumb to the drum when the drum meet them. You feel it...

Although many dancehall rhythms are very digital, the source of many of these rhythms is right from the beginning of time.

Although the rhythm tracks sound a little bit modern, there is a source and a well that they all go back to, which

is the fountain of music, the root of the music - which is the one drop. And they have to feel it in the one drop. For there is 360 degrees in the circle.

When you mention 'the one drop' I automatically think of the 'One Drop' of Bob Marley: what do you think of Bob?

Bob Marley a legend, you know.
And legends speak for themselves through music.

What was it like growing up in Denham Town?

All my school days was in Denham Town or Barbican. I went

to Denham Town secondary school. Which is in a downtown region. And downtown used to be much nicer than it is today - much cooler and much calmer. Even though the same political nonsense used to go on. I have seen it all before - the calm before the storm, and after the storm. Jah live.

What was your background?

I come from one of the poorest houses. My father is a man who used to do labourer

work, making tiles in a factory named Moore Brothers. And my mother is a diehard independent hustler: a higgler - she sell ground provisions and stuff like that, a farmer who till the soil so we can't starve. So because of this firm upbringing and firm mentors in our background of the role mother and father play, we grow to be firm in our headspace and know what it takes to survive in the rough world we live in.

Having a mother who was a higgler would seem to be very useful training for the music business...

Man learn the survival route through
those means and channels.

How did you come to make 'The Ruler' for Robert French in 1986?

It was a rainy day and a producer by the

name of Robert French was working inside Penthouse studios. I came out of my house without one dime flat against another and I went up to Blue Mountain recording studio which is situated at 2B Grove Road. I met a man who always has been giving me certain instruction about the music and how certain things operate, for you have such men designed to do these works. When the rain was falling an entertainer by the name of Clement Irie came to the studio and was going to Penthouse to record for Mr Robert French.

And even though the rain was falling I say, "Jah Bless", and go with him. And Mr French give me this tune and I just give it one lick, one time, red light; and yeah man, I just pass the test.

Where did you develop your vocal growl?

Through the passage of time the vocal develop, because this is our trade and our art and if you don't master your art and your trade, you must fade.

Did people compare you to Shabba?

No comparison: people compare it to Shabba, to this man, to that man. But at the end of the day we still all our own - all our own come out of we that we have to do. Most importantly.

Tell me about songs like 'Tribal War' and 'Murderer' - very strong songs.

A song like 'Tribal War' come of a sticky time in a Jamdown way. Election approach and we know that we is treated as pawns. And 'Murderer' is about nonsense war that we do perpetrate towards our own selves. 'Murderer' is about the death of my friend - and your friend, his friend, next man friend. **Murderation.**

You have recorded a number of songs that almost define dancehall. How do you feel about that?

It just the greatness within the music. And I and I was chosen by the Almighty One to come and establish that sound in that time. That sound in this time need more positivity, because nuff man tek it as a joyride and it is leading a whole generation and a whole nation astray. **So we have to go back even to the roots,** to them era there. Because the music have gone to a point where it have to be saying something on a level.

People want the positivity more than anything else. People are hungry for the positiveness, to make them forget the stress and help them get in touch with themselves - with their inner self and reality. Everyone love truth and rights, even when they make it as a fight. Only the fittest of the fittest will survive - **only those who are in the know in this information age.**

Almost unnoticed, reggae music has spread across and around the world until it has become part of the very fabric of global culture. Regarded with racist condescension by all but a few in the late 1960s, a decade later the notion of Jamaican music was inextricably interwoven around the image of Bob Marley, who held aloft the red, gold and green banner of Rastafari.

REGGAE

Marley's success opened the ears of his fans to a piratical treasure trove of some of the most heartfelt and moving music of the last century. To those already attuned to the culture of Jamaican music, it came as no surprise that the sound system deejays and the wizards of dub should have provided the template for rap music.

In some quarters it has been fashionable to somehow suggest that Marley's enormous popularity means he was never really representative of reggae and therefore not truly cool. Yet the lie is given to such a specious argument when you find yourself in obscure African or Asian

OUTER-NATIONAL

backwaters and suddenly encounter giant murals of the Tuff Gong. As he knew only too well, it was Bob's job to open up the world's headspace to the music of truth and rights (and love and heartbreak) of reggae. Without his so admirably having fulfilled his task, you wouldn't even be looking at this book.

"I only played those reggae records at the Roxy because there weren't enough punk records to play," said Don Letts, whose record-spinning at the Roxy is always said to have led to the punk-reggae fusion celebrated in Bob Marley's 'Punky Reggae Party', released in 1977.

At the Roxy and other punk clubs and shows, there was a ready white audience for reggae. In the barren musical time that was the pre-punk 1970s, reggae was one of the only forms of music that was consistently creative and inspiring. When Chris Blackwell had signed Bob Marley he had been aware that, after a period of great innovation, rock music was declining in interest. The first records by the Wailers helped fill this gap; in the soundtrack for the film *The Harder They Come*, there already existed the quintessential reggae primer; and as well as *Catch A Fire* and *Burnin'*, the radical chic who had turned on to that record had branched out to Toots and the Maytals' *Funky Kingston* LP and Burning Spear's *Marcus Garvey* album; a few brave souls would even venture to the Daddy Kool record shop in London's West End to pick up copies of the latest Jamaican *pre's*, short - somewhat oxymoronically - for pre-release, as reggae imports were known.

The curious poetry of Rastafari appealed to punks on both sides of the Atlantic: in New York poetess Patti Smith espoused the music of Tapper Zukie, bringing him and Don Letts onstage together when she played at London's Hammersmith Odeon in 1977.

When John 'Johnny Rotten' Lydon broke a long interview silence on a programme on London's Capital Radio, he had included several magnificent reggae records: Augustus Pablo's 'King Tubby Meets the Rockers Uptown', Culture's 'I'm Not Ashamed', Aswad's 'Jah Wonderful', and songs by Ken Boothe, the Gladiators, and Fred Locks, as well as Dr Alimantado's inspirational 'Born For A Purpose'; every one a winner.

It was the rhythm of reggae - whether you could hear it

The 2-Tone movement of the late 1970s was a natural outgrowth of the punk-reggae fusion. Thanks to Jerry Dammers, the leader of the Specials (pictured right at a characteristically sedate show) and 2-Tone, the galloping beat of ska music was all over the UK charts in 1979 and 1980. The Clash (above), meanwhile, had co-opted reggae into their set ever since they recorded their own version of Junior Murvin's 'Police And Thieves'; later they did the same for Willie Williams' 'Armagideon Time'.

in specific songs or not - that was the heartbeat of the Clash. Reggae was certainly the coolest music to be into in 1975 and 1976 - largely because it seemed the only form that was progressing in any way - and it was just one more of the right credentials for the Clash.

The Clash were the first group to integrate Jamaican sounds fully into their music. On record reggae's rhythms were first taken up by the Clash, who to great effect bravely interpreted Junior Murvin's 'Police and Thieves', a reggae classic of 1976, on their first LP. Later the Clash were to re-work Toots Hibbert's 'Pressure Drop' and Willie Williams' masterly 'Armagideon Time'; at a rehearsal for the *London Calling* stage-show, Joe Strummer ran through John Holt's then-current hit 'OK Fred', and snatches of it would be dropped into the live set.

Clash vocalist Joe Strummer had been into reggae for a long time, ever since Mole from the 101'ers - the pub-rock group he had been a member of prior to the Clash - had turned him onto it by non-stop playing of Big Youth's *Screaming Target* LP. When the Clash recorded 'Police And Thieves' he was at first nervous of seeming 'naff', the 1977 equivalent of white-men-play-the-blues. How could Joe possibly emulate Junior Murvin's feathery voice, he wondered.

Yet 'Police And Thieves' became the standard bearer for the reggae/punk crossover that was chronicled in Bob Marley's 'Punky Reggae Party', produced by Lee 'Scratch' Perry, who'd done the same job on the Murvin record, as well as the Clash's 'Complete Control' single: "We were looking for a reggae production, but he wanted to learn how to do a punk production," said Joe.

By the time they played Bond's in Manhattan in 1981, which kicked the group up to an almost legendary level in the USA, much of the set seemed to consist of sprawling dub, as though you were listening to a sound system in one of London's Jamaican shebeens.

In the middle of 1978, when out playing the *On Parole* tour, Joe Strummer had admitted to stepping backwards through the Jamaican music he loved towards ska, the largely instrumental sound that had roughly coincided with the island's independence. Perhaps this was not so surprising: opening the show, and having a miserable time finding sleeping accommodation, was a group from Coventry called the Special Aka (who quickly became, more simply, the Specials), another set of protégés from Bernie Rhodes, the manager of the Clash. And the musical specialty of the Special AKA was ska.

Just as the Rolling Stones had co-opted and rewritten black American rhythm'n'blues, 2-Tone was an art-school interpretation of another form. Jerry Dammers, a vicar's son whose project 2-Tone was, emerged from the same English art school system that had inspired John Lennon, Ray Davies, Keith Richards and the Clash. Although there was therefore a sense that his group the Specials were playing out a version of art-school gangsters ('Gangsters', ironically, was the title of the first Specials single), the movement all the same had its roots in Dammers' experience of life in the multi-racial English Midlands city of Coventry.

In the late 1970s Britain was riven with undercurrents of racial strife: both Rock Against Racism and the Anti-Nazi League, which had been born at the same time as

Linton Kwesi Johnson (pictured left - and opposite top right in the Brixton office of the Race Today organisation, with Darcus Howe, his militant spar) set the agenda for the style that became known as Dub Poetry.
In Jamaica artists like Oku Onuora and the late Michael Smith similarly took up the mike for the purpose of word-power. Benjamin Zephaniah, (middle left) meanwhile, has moved the form along in the UK.
Middle right: The Police's Sting and Stewart Copeland with Steel Pulse.

punk, moved in their somewhat self-righteous manners to combat this. But shows by 2-Tone's multi-racial acts - especially those by the Specials - displayed a level of paradox of which Samuel Beckett would have been proud: for reasons that were hard to fathom, England's racist skinheads had decided that the group was their own.

Like SS stormtroopers, packs of skins would invade the stage wherever the group played, remaining shoulder-to-shoulder with the musicians throughout the set, causing genuine psychological concerns for Dammers and his crew. Later this was cited as a principal reason for the group breaking up after only two albums.

Whilst Coventry had supplied the Specials and Selecter, Birmingham provided the Beat and Dexy's Midnight

Runners. The same city also gave birth to UB40, whose base sound was reggae and rocksteady rather than ska - determinedly independent in the finest punk example, they would gradually grow and grow until they became one of Britain's biggest exports.

Whilst purist white reggae fans in the UK chose to deride them, the people of Jamaica took them to their collective heart, and as the years went on IRIE-FM, the Jamaican reggae station, would play UB40 albums in their entirety.

Even more than the Clash, the group that most successfully co-opted the rhythm of reggae into their sound was the Police. By the early 1980s they had become

the biggest group in the world. How did it happen? "We were in a curious position," observed Sting, the group's singer. "Because of how old we were, and the experiences we'd had, we could be fairly objective about the whole thing.

"I could see that punk was going to develop in some way. It was obvious that if you could ally that energy and that drive to a more musical form, it would be dynamite. And what I wanted to have was energy rock'n'roll allied to harmonic, melodic music. Through listening to the various songs you can see how my writing gradually becomes more sinuous. There's a reggae element in 'Don't Stand So Close To Me', but you can hardly hear it. The music flows more now – there's hardly any breaks."

"What I started off doing was structuring songs that had an eight-bar section of rock'n'roll coupled with, say, sixteen bars of reggae. Which, in fact, you can see in 'Roxanne'." STING

The foundations of Island Records lay in Jamaican music, and the label's catalogue was an established part of UK music. In 1975, however, in a sign of the way that the wind was blowing, Virgin Records in London set up its own reggae label, Front Line, with strong initial releases from the Mighty Diamonds and U-Roy. At the beginning of 1978 Richard Branson, the Virgin owner, was to be found in Kingston on a signing spree that brought Culture, I-Roy, and many other acts to the label.

Gradually, it emerged that these acts were intended for other markets than Britain. There was, it seemed, a large appetite for Jamaican music in West Africa. This, one discovered, lay behind the Virgin team's assiduous efforts to sign up every reggae act they could lay their hands on. Nigeria, the largest of all West African states, already had its own reggae star in Sonny Okusuns, who blended reggae with highlife and juju.

Enthusiasm for reggae was not restricted only to the Third World. One of the biggest Jamaican stars in Africa was Jimmy Cliff. In Brazil, where he lived for much of the time, he was an even bigger star.

At the same time as versions of reggae were emerging in such developing countries, the most advanced, affluent nation in the world was giving birth to a new music whose roots were in a specific Jamaican form. Hiphop music is now recognised as having been a direct descendant of the Jamaican art of deejaying - even though

In the second half of the 1970s Aswad (left) managed to be both the toughest and most musical manifestation of English reggae: it was a shame their sound had to soften in the next decade to gain a seemingly unending stream of hits. Meanwhile, Birmingham's Steel Pulse (below) never softened their tone: led by the elaborately locksed David Hinds, their Handsworth Revolution and Tribute To The Martyrs albums were masterly: when the market for them dried up in the UK, they worked in other territories, notably the United States, where they had considerable success... although not as much as UB40 (right), also from Birmingham, who by dint of their laid-back perseverance managed quietly to become one of the biggest-selling groups in the world.

Party time and music came to the streets of London with the birth of the Notting Hill Carnival, now the biggest street carnival in Western Europe.

Normally reserved Londoners were to be seen dancing in the streets. Even the upright British Bobby would link arms with some scantily-clad Caribbean beauty, helmet swapped for head dress. Though never without some incident the Carnival was a generally safer place than most football matches.

NOTTING HILL GATE

much of that form itself came directly from the eccentric between-record raps of US radio DJs, and from iconoclasts like the Last Poets. MC Kool Herc, a Jamaican deejay who set up a sound system in the Bronx during the mid-1970s, is widely acknowledged as having been a forerunner of rap. And the Jamaican parentage of artists like Biggie Smalls and KRS-1 was a formative influence on their styles; New York-based acts like Shinehead and Shaggy adhered more closely to Jamaican forms.

Many Jamaican artists have kept themselves alive with lucrative 'revival' tours of Japan, where ska has proved particularly popular, spawning its own local groups. Even in places like Indonesia's Bali, Jamaican music is lapped up, perhaps in part because the island has three factories that produce red, gold and green 'reggae' clothing. In Australia, meanwhile, the aborigine reggae group No Fixed Address for long held popular sway. In the south-west of the United States, the Hopi tribe of Native Americans has a close empathy with reggae culture in general and the work of Bob Marley in particular. Reggae also seemed to appeal to the dispossessed dwelling in the former Soviet Union and its empire: Poland, for example, seemed very partial to the rhythms of the Isle of Springs. And in the 1990s the Drum & Bass and Jungle styles have clearly stated the extent to which Jamaican music has become a staple influence on UK club culture.

During the late 1970s, the energy and charisma of Bob Marley began to filter through Africa. By the end of the 20th century images of Bob Marley were omnipresent throughout Africa, from Dakar to Lagos, Cape Town to Cairo: Africa Unite, indeed! In the Ivory Coast, Alpha Blondy sold huge quantities of cassettes - despite the fact that, when he returned from New York to inform his parents of his belief in Rastafari, they had had him placed under psychiatric help. In 1986 he recorded in Jamaica, with backing by the Wailers. Influenced by the influences on Blondy, who he had worked with whilst living in the Ivory Coast, was Mali's Askia Mobido.

Also from the Ivory Coast, Tangara Speed Ghoda blended reggae with local forms. In South Africa, then under the yoke of apartheid, Lucky Dube similarly took up the reggae beat and Rasta influence. Unsurprisingly, his first album, *Rasta Never Die*, released in 1985, was banned by the apartheid rulers. Senzo Mthetwa combined reggae with both the country's *mbaganga* tradition and gospel. Elsewhere, Zimbabwe's Thomas Mapfumo, Ghana's African Brothers, and Nigeria's Mandators brought Jamaican sounds to their native musics.

It was hardly surprising; Africa, after all, was where it had all begun.

Is the raucous delivery of American rap star Busta Rhymes a genetic throwback to the Jamaican origins of his parents? Whatever, a considerable number of US rappers - including the late Biggie 'Notorious B.I.G.' Smalls - could trace their origin to the Isle of Springs. Did MC Kool Herc have any inkling what he was starting?

Above: Baaba Maal, the West African superstar, with conscious king Luciano in Senegal.

Luciano (right) wears the shackles that bound the feet of the millions of slaves who passed through the processing centre on Goree Island, in the harbour of Dakar, the Senegalese capital.

When Jimmy Cliff travelled to Senegal, he heard music that for him showed precisely that reggae had emerged from the heart of Africa. The wonderful music of Senegal's great Baaba Maal encompasses a myriad African styles. And it was a profound moment for Luciano when, with Sizzla (in red) he met Maal in the west African country in 1998.

ReggaeXplosion: THE EXHIBITION

This book was produced in collaboration with ReggaeXplosion, an international touring exhibition, which provided a visual archive from which to select photographs. Researched and designed by Adrian Boot and Shelley Warren with editorial from Chris Salewicz and help from reggae fans and professionals worldwide, the exhibition brought together a stunning collection of images, record memorabilia, sound and audio-visual material charting 50 years of Jamaican music. The aim of the exhibition was and is to provide a visually exciting and informative insight into this ever important musical genre. Produced and toured by Exhibitz, the exhibition was staged at the Roundhouse, London in October 2000, having already appeared in Birmingham, Liverpool, Sheffield and Leeds. Through support from the Millennium Commission a series of workshops and an educational CDRom were produced for each exhibition venue.

ReggaeXplosion will be touring worldwide for the forseeable future. For further information about the exhibition or print sales please contact Shelley Warren at exhibitz@netcomuk.co.uk or visit www.reggaexplosion.co.uk

COPYRIGHT CREDITS

PHOTOGRAPHERS

TIM BARROW

Tim Barrow studied for four years at Plymouth College of Art and Design specialising in underwater photography, an interest he derived from an active career in surfing. Although he surfed for Great Britain his interest in photography led him to London where he worked from 1978 at Black Echoes and as a freelancer for other clients and publications. Never far from the sea, Tim lives in Barnstaple and continues to surf and think.

ADRIAN BOOT

Adrian Boot graduated from Surrey University before moving to Jamaica to teach physics in the early 1970s, returning to Britain to freelance for the NME, Melody Maker, The Times and The Guardian. By the mid-1970s he had become staff photographer for Melody Maker. Moving on, he has been chief photographer for Live Aid; for Nelson Mandela: Freedom at 70; for Roger Water's The Wall in Berlin; for Greenpeace in the former Soviet Union. He has also worked with ORBIS, the flying eye hospital, in Africa; the British Council in Iraq and Jordan; and for the Grateful Dead in Egypt; as well as for Island Records in Jamaica, Colombia and many parts of the world. His books include Jah Revenge and Babylon On a Thin Wire (both with Michael Thomas), and Bob Marley: Songs Of Freedom (with Chris Salewicz), & International Reggae (with Peter Simon). Since building his own computer in 1976, Boot has been increasingly involved in computer technology and photography, DVD and internet technology.

ROB HANN

Self-taught Rob Hann began working as a photographer at the age of 38. Specialising in portraiture he has contributed to NME, The Times, Independent on Sunday Review, Scotland On Sunday Magazine, Straight No Chaser, Time Out and The Big Issue among many others. The Busta Rhymes picture was shot backstage in Cleveland, Ohio for NME in November 1997. "I was told I had one minute to do the session."

DAVE HENDLEY

"I first travelled to Kingston, Jamaica in the spring of 1977. As a fanatical reggae fan I was primarily on a mission to fill in the gaps in my record collection and to visit the home of the music I loved. At that time I was also writing the reggae page for Blues & Soul and had the additional task of doing as many interviews as I could. The singers, players and producers I encountered during that trip were so very welcoming and generous with their time, in particular King Tubby, Prince Jammy, Dr Alimantado, Jojo Hookim, Errol Thompson, Lee Perry, Tappa Zukie, Earl Zero, Yabby You and Coxsone Dodd. Photography was not really a very high priority and I remember being acutely aware of not letting the pursuit of pictures spoil my trip. The camera can often create a barrier between people and I reasoned that I was in Jamaica as a lover of the music, not as a photographer. It never dawned on me that there would be any interest in these images nearly a quarter of a century later - I now really wish that I had taken a few more."

PHOTOGRAPHERS

ACKNOWLEDGMENTS

BETH LESSER

Much of Beth Lesser's photographic work covered the dancehall scene in Kingston in the 1980s, focussing on singers, deejays, selecters and sound system operators. While in Jamaica she would often be found at Jammy's studio, Channel One, Youth Promotion and Black Scorpio - "Some of my favourite pictures are shots of local hangers-on who just showed up in music places hoping for a break." Now living in Toronto, Beth continues taking pictures and also produces Reggae Quarterly which is distributed world-wide.

PETER MURPHY

Peter Murphy's photographic career with Claire Hershman began because he knew the music and she had the equipment. They sold their first ever set of photographs for a rushed-out minor label live reggae album. They spent the 1970s indulging in their twin passions, music and travel. The music provided a direct route to the heartbeat of societies as far flung as Jamaica and Nigeria. In 1986 Murphy was lighting cameraman for the award winning dramas Passing Glory and Before I Die Forever. Murphy handled the same role for the title sequence of the first Batman movie.

JEAN BERNARD SOHIEZ

"It was the mid-Seventies and I was looking for something new... something to satisfy my soul... and then I discovered Natty Dread. Bob Marley changed my life", laughs Jean Bernard Sohiez. He packed his Leica, abandoned Paris and headed off to London to cover the reggae scene. He already contributed to France's premier music mag, Rock Et Folk, and once in London, through NME editor Neil Spencer, began to get regular photographic commissions. Jean Bernard joined forces with freelance writer Paul Bradshaw and on the reggae underground acquired the nickname of 'Frenchie'. He was a regular at the sound system dances of Coxsone Outernational, Jah Shaka, Fatman Hi-Fi et al and anyone passing through town came into focus via his camera. He visited Jamaica for the first time in 1980 and most recently in 1999. While best known for his reggae portraits he has received acclaim in France for his portraits of a new generation of painters - 'la nouvelle expression libre' - like Jean Charles Blais and Francois Boisrond. In 2001 Jean Bernard is resident in Paris, working on several personal projects, contributes to Straight No Chaser and still loves JA's 'old school'.

WAYNE TIPPETTS

Wayne Tippetts, born in England in 1959, studied Documentary Photography at North East London Polytechnic. Graduating in 1986, he started to visit Jamaica, travelling the island, taking photographs that ranged from religion to the race track and dance hall culture. A selection of his black and white photographs was shown in Kingston, Jamaica at the Grosvenor Gallery in 1994. In 1993 Wayne decided to live and work as a photographer in Jamaica, where he taught photography at the Edna Manley school for Visual Art in Kingston. His dancehall photographs have been published as record sleeves and magazine features.

In addition to the photographers and writers who have contributed directly to this book, many people have provided support, sympathy, hard work and ideas during the development of the ReggaeXplosion exhibition. Thanks to: Simon Buckland, Giles Moberly, Neville Garrick, David Rodigan, Hulton Getty, Retna, Redferns, Camera Press, Black Echoes and 56 Hope Road Music Ltd for contributing their images; Gaylene Martin, and Gaz Mayall for access to their impressive record collections and expert advice. To Vicky Fox, a superb re-toucher, production assistant and general punk priestess, a big thanks for help and laughter through the past few years; Jeremy Collingwood proved far more than an avid supporter of reggae: from priceless contacts to endless advice and provision of the rarest memorabilia we are ever grateful. Utmost respect to Val Wilson at the Camden Mix without whose hard work and support none of this would have happened; to those in the music business, grateful thanks to Ian Snodgrass at Universal Island, Mark Marot, Mark Le Goy and Laura Gladman, Pete Holdsworth at Pressure Sounds, Adrian Sherwood at On-U Sounds, Bob Harding at Blood & Fire, Chris Cracknell, Peade & Tony McDermott at Greensleeves, Chris Lane at Fashion, Lol, Noel and John at Dub Vendor and Simon Dornan at Virgin Megastores. Thanks to the Roundhouse crew of Kevin Luton and the Roundhouse staff, especially Phoenix and Amanda for their daily enthusiasm, Geoff and Judy at Jamaica Blue, Leeds Photovisual, Microvideo, Marie at VSC Camden, the Jamaican High Commission, Intro, Stylorouge, Zak, Eira and Rob Warren and Helmut Teichert-Kuhr. Respect to Paul Clarke and Peter Harvey at the London School of Printing and their prodigy Sonia, Matt, Dan and Phil for their films and enthusiasm. To Jo Bloom, Miss P, Nicky Ezer, Time Out and London Live for getting the word out; Mykaell Riley, Paul Bradshaw, Don Letts, Steve Barrow, Linton Kwesi Johnson, Andrew Neale and Penny Reel. To the Roundhouse Trust, Rachael Mulhearn at Liverpool Maritime Museum, Steve Byfield at Leeds Leisure Services, everyone at the Birmingham Drum, Sam Irani at NCPM, and Fiona Drury at Write Angle for co-ordinating the Australasian tour.

For their invaluable aid towards both the exhibition and the book, serious respect is due to Ann Hodges, Roger Brown, Justine Henzell, Island Communications, Rita Marley, Julian Alexander, Steve Barrow and the Rougher than Rough crew, Humphrey Pryce, Suzette Newman, Mark Painter, and Verrah Senton and Trevor Wyatt.

Any attempt to list all those people that have contributed to the project over the years would be impossible without committing grave errors. The Editors of this book and Exhibitz would like to apologise for any omissions. No-one is worth more than anyone else.

INDEX

Index to people and artists who appear in the text of Reggae Explosion